MENTORING MATTERS

What Every Mentor Needs to Know

D0166980

TOM OSBORNE

FOREWORD BY CAREY CASEY
NATIONAL CENTER FOR FATHERING

TEAMMATES®
MENTORING PROGRAM

Together We Transform Lives

DEDICATION

Together We Transform Lives
To be a **Mentor**, contact teammates.org
1-877-531-8326 (TEAM)

Mentoring Matters:
What Every Mentor Needs to Know

Tom Osborne

Together We Transform Lives
TEAMMATES
MENTORING

ACKNOWLEDGMENTS

I would like to thank Nancy Osborne and Barbara Hopkins for their role in starting Teammates in 1991 with twenty two football players and their mentees.

Thanks also to Suzanne Hince and her excellent staff for their efforts in expanding Teammates and transforming it into an excellent organization.

Finally, thanks to the thousands of mentors who volunteer their time and their hearts with their mentees as they make this a better world.

FOREWORD

December 19, 1977, Memphis, Tennessee. Nebraska vs. North Carolina in the Liberty Bowl.

I was a tailback for North Carolina, and although I was in the game for some plays, I didn't get any touches that day. Our defense played great, and our offense did enough to get a lead on the Cornhuskers. But Nebraska's back-up quarterback threw two touchdown passes in the fourth quarter to beat us, 21-17.

After the game, I was sitting on one of our team's four buses, waiting to leave. As a junior, I had some optimism because we had a lot of good players coming back, and we'd be fine next year, but many of the seniors were almost in tears. The bus was almost silent.

Then I heard a voice from the front of the bus, and I looked up to see a man in red standing there. Tom Osborne. I'm sure he was the last person most of the other players wanted to see at that moment. He had just beaten us, and now he was coming to rub it in? No, I knew that wasn't what Coach Osborne was about.

I don't remember his exact words, but he sincerely told us that we played well and he appreciated the opportunity to compete against us.

I was already very active in FCA, and that's where I learned some things about Coach Osborne. Thanks to a knee injury and God's calling on my life, I later worked full-time for FCA and had the pleasure of being with Coach and his family on numerous occasions.

Today God has led both of us to address a critical issue in our nation and in the world: *too many children growing up without a healthy father or father figure.* I know Coach has seen that crisis play out in the lives of numerous young men, and *Mentoring Matters* is a clear call for more of us engaged, responsible men to invest with passion and purpose into young people who need us.

What does that look like for you? There are plenty of helpful tips right in this book, but here's a powerful example our team members at the National Center for Fathering heard about not long ago:

Omar is a dad who was at a swimming pool with his family one hot summer day. There was a young boy playing with his sister nearby. Several times Omar heard the sister say, "You're playing too rough with me." The boy replied, "There is no one else."

Omar heard that comment, and it sparked something inside of him. He thought, *Well, if that little guy needs someone to roughhouse with, I can do that.* And roughhouse they did.

While Omar splashed and goofed around with his own kids, he naturally and easily began to include this other young boy. Between splash attacks, he found a moment to talk with the boy about some of the ways young men need to act, like treating their mothers and sisters with respect and kindness.

Across the way, Omar's wife was talking with the boy's mother, and Omar later learned that she thanked his wife for sharing Omar at the pool. The boy's father was not in the picture, and she knew he needed positive role models. Omar was glad he could provide those brief moments of fun and invest a little in his life.

That's the end of the story until the next fall. Omar was volunteering at his children's school as part of our WATCH D.O.G.S. (Dads Of Great Students) program. As he was walking the halls and helping in different classrooms, he saw that little boy again. Without any prompting, the boy walked up to Omar and said, "I am still being good to my sister." Omar says they have bumped into each other at the school several times since.

I hope that story inspires you like it does me. I often challenge dads to encourage other kids outside their home, and it doesn't have to involve a huge commitment of time and energy. Even little gestures and comments can go a long way. Omar simply showed that he cared, and those brief moments of interaction at the pool made a lasting impression on that boy. It's heroic stuff!

As Omar wrote to us, "There are children in our community who need us. To any dad out there, please keep your eyes and ears open, and do what comes natural."

Being a mentor is a high calling, but it's something all of us can do. There are kids around you who need your roughhousing . . . your encouragement . . . your challenge to be kind and respectful. So, please, as you read the great ideas in this book, start looking around you. And then just do what comes natural.

Carey Casey
CEO, National Center for Fathering

CONTENTS

INTRODUCTION

I was only four years old, but I knew something significant had happened. It was December 7, 1941, and my father and I were sitting in my grandparents' living room on a Sunday afternoon when the radio broadcast came over the air describing the Japanese attack on Pearl Harbor. The reason I knew something extraordinary had happened wasn't that I comprehended what was occurring in Hawaii, but rather my father's reaction. He jumped out of his chair and announced that he "was going to get into this thing." I knew he was angry and excited, but I wasn't fully aware of the significance of what was happening to me and my family until later. My dad was beyond draft age and had a wife and two children, so he didn't have to get involved. However, he was very patriotic, had a strong sense of responsibility and felt compelled to do his part. So he volunteered to join the army, going in as a captain in charge of an ordinance unit composed largely of auto mechanics and repair men from his place of business, an automobile dealership and repair shop. A few other men from nearby towns in the central part of Nebraska were also included in his company.

Little did I know he would be gone for more than four years, that my mother, my brother Jack and I would move to the small town of St. Paul, Nebraska to live with my maternal grandparents, and my world would literally be turned upside-down. St. Paul was fifty miles north of our home in Hastings. A mid-sized town of more than twenty thousand, Hastings had a college and a fair amount of industry and commerce; St. Paul had less than two thousand people, was located near the Loup River and was almost entirely dedicated to serving the agricultural community of the area. My maternal grandfather had been a fairly prosperous farmer but had lost both of his farms during the depression and had taken a job as a meat cutter at the local locker plant. He worked six days a week, and I remember the weekly pay check which he gave to my grandmother on Saturday nights was $49.50. We lived on the edge of town with five or six milk cows and a few chickens and pigs. My grandfather delivered milk and butter to a few customers each morning before he went to work. So life was slower and settled into a rhythm as I entered kindergarten for my first year of school.

People realized our nation was now involved in a global conflict; playing was for all the marbles. Losing the war would be catastrophic as it would result in subjugation to the Axis forces. Everyone became engaged in some capacity, contributing in ways such as planting "victory gardens" to supplement food supplies so there were adequate rations for our troops. Butter, meat and gasoline were rationed. Cars were limited to speeds of forty five miles per hour to conserve fuel. Our elementary school gathered scrap iron to be converted into military vehicles. My mother, a school teacher before she married and a full time mother after Jack and I were born, took a job in an ammunition plant in Grand Island, located twenty two miles south of St. Paul. She came home every evening with explosive compounds splattered on her work boots. I was impressed with the way those drops of TNT would flare up and pop when you lit a match to them. She also came home and cried every night when there was no letter from my dad. There were many such nights during the Battle of the Bulge when communication was cut off. The war exacted a toll on everyone, especially those who were left behind.

I remember the day I stood in the yard of my grandparents' home and watched the clouds of smoke rise from an explosion in the ammunitions plant where my mother worked. Many people were killed that day–fortunately my mom wasn't one of them. When my dad heard about the explosion he insisted that my mother quit working there so "at least one of them would survive the war." She went back to teaching school, but the anxiety about my dad never went away. Much later in life, at age seventy two, she would suffer a massive stroke. I believe this may have been triggered by the anxiety she felt when my dad went with some of his fellow soldiers to retrace their steps through France, Belgium and Germany. His return to Europe seemed to awaken old anxieties and stresses in her life which had never been completely put to rest. She spoke of his departure on the trip to Europe as though she felt that he would never return. Unfortunately he did return, but not to find the same wife he had been married to for many years. The stroke left her partially paralyzed and unable to speak

During those World War II years, I recall feeling inadequate and abandoned in that I was the only child in my class I can recall who didn't have a father present. My classmates' fathers were still at home with them as they were exempt from the draft due to age and family responsibilities. I knew I had a father, that he loved me and that he was engaged in a noble cause, but I still sensed something important was missing. I felt somehow inferior and of less value than other children. I also remember having trouble getting to sleep at night and having nightmares of Nazi soldiers marching down the streets of St. Paul. The war and my father's absence, coupled with my mother's anxiety over his fate left its mark.

The reason I have spent time reflecting on the past as I begin this book about mentoring is that those experiences I had more than seventy years ago are being replicated in the lives of many young people today. We are not engaged in a world war, but many of our children are experiencing father absence, and many are living in stressful situations. Some have no parents. Many are dealing with disruption of their personal lives and are anxious and uncertain about the future.

William Bennett, in 2001 published the book *The Broken Hearth*. He wrote: "the nuclear family, defined as a monogamous married couple living with their children, is vital to civilization's success." He goes on to point out the alarming increase in single-parent families, fatherlessness, divorce and cohabitation. What was true in 2001 is even more pronounced and concerning today. More than half of our children are growing up without both biological parents. This means a large number of our young people have experienced significant trauma during their childhoods. Separation from a parent through death, divorce, a war or incarceration always leaves a wound, which sometimes never completely heals.

During those turbulent years of 1941 through 1945 I clearly could have benefited from a mentor in my life. I was very fortunate to find one in my uncle, Virgil Welsh, who lived across the street. Virgil was a banker and an avid outdoorsman. He took an interest in me and taught me to catch catfish in the Loup River, hunt for pheasants and ducks, swim, and gather gooseberries and chokecherries which my grandmother made into jelly. He even taught me how to make a bow from a dogwood branch because I badly wanted to perfect my archery skills after reading *Robin Hood*. I remember cold January nights when we would visit his trap lines to see if he had captured any mink, beaver or muskrats. Fur coats were popular in those days, and he supplemented his income by trapping.

Having someone care about me, invest time in me and serve as a male role model during those years was critical to my development. The experience of having a mentor when my dad was absent made a significant difference in my life, and throughout the years I've tried to do the same for the young people with whom I've worked. This book will give you insight on my journey and hopefully encourage you to grow as a mentor.

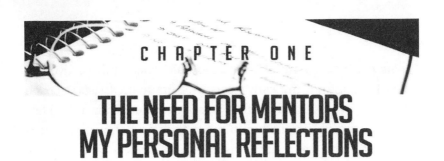

CHAPTER ONE

THE NEED FOR MENTORS
MY PERSONAL REFLECTIONS

My experience during World War II parallels the story of Telemachus, the son of Odysseus, the main character in Homer's epic *The Odyssey*. Odysseus leaves to fight in the Trojan war entrusting his whole household, including his son Telemachus, to his old friend Mentor. The Odyssey was written in approximately 1000 BC. Roughly 2700 years later Francois Fenelon wrote *Les Adventures de Telemaque,* a continuation of Homer's *Odyssey,* which expanded and clarified the role of Mentor in the life of Telemachus. Fenelon portrays Mentor as a wise counselor, advisor, teacher and role model who plays a major role in developing Telemachus into a fine young man in his father's absence. The Mentor portrayed by Fenelon exemplifies what we have come to know as a "mentor" today.

Throughout history mentors have aided the growth and maturation of young people just as Mentor did in literary works long ago. However, there have been few periods in time where mentors were needed more than today.

Early in our nation's history young men often worked beside their fathers on farms, in trades and small businesses. Girls often assisted their mothers in cooking, gardening and household chores. Families usually took their meals together. The great majority of families was intact unless one of the parents was deceased. There was a great deal of personal interaction and communication between parents and children.

Things have changed. I witnessed many of those changes

taking place during my time as a football coach at the University of Nebraska, from my early years as a graduate assistant coach beginning in 1962 until my final year as head coach in 1997. During those years I worked with more than two thousand young men. I traveled the country visiting high schools and sitting in living rooms visiting families of players we were recruiting. Some of our recruits lived in affluent areas and went to nice schools, and some were in the inner city and lived in tenements. They came from rural and urban areas, and they represented many different ethnic groups.

There is no question that things were very different in 1962 than they are today. The biggest change I saw during my years as a coach involved family structure and stability. According to the United States Census Bureau, the number of single parent families has tripled since the 1960s. At the time it was relatively rare to encounter the family of a recruit that was not intact, with a father and a mother living in the same home as the young man I was recruiting. As time went on, however, I encountered young men living in single parent households more and more frequently. Usually these homes had a mother present but no father.

It also became more and more common to have to visit parents in two different places if both were involved in their son's life, but all too frequently the father was not even mentioned and was of little or no consequence in the player's decision concerning what school he should attend. Fatherlessness became much more common and made coaching more challenging.

A young man raised without a father was usually prone to a great many more difficulties than a player coming from a two parent, stable home. A fatherless child is twice as likely to be jailed or be placed in juvenile detention, is much more likely to drop out of school, is more likely to be involved in a teenage pregnancy, is more prone to substance abuse, and is more disposed to mental and emotional illness. I also noticed that fatherless players were often more difficult to coach as they seemed to be less willing to accept authority and often were not as disciplined in their approach to athletics and academics.

Of course there were exceptions. There were those who, despite family instability, were exemplary student-athletes, but by and large fatherlessness was a problem which became more pronounced with the passage of time. Young women raised without fathers are negatively impacted by father absence much the same as boys. They are more apt to have difficulty with the law, drop out of school, have pregnancies outside of marriage, engage in substance abuse and suffer from higher incidences of emotional and mental illness.

It is estimated that there are between twenty to thirty million fatherless children in the United States today, roughly one third of all children. The percentage living without biological fathers is much higher (more than half), as many now live with stepfathers. Sometimes stepfathers are not as devoted to children as their biological fathers, but again there are many exceptions.

Stephen Baskerville, a professor at Howard University, says "Virtually every major personal and social pathology can be traced to fatherlessness more than to any other single factor. Fatherlessness far surpasses both poverty and race as a predictor of social deviance." My experience as a coach is consistent with Baskerville's observation.

I was interested in a story told by Dr. Wade Horn, President of the National Fatherhood Initiative. Dr. Horn referred to an effort to reduce the elephant herd in Kruger National Park in South Africa, as the numbers of elephants exceeded the food supply. There were not enough trees to keep the elephants fed. A decision was made to relocate some of the elephants to Pilanesburg National Park by helicopter. Adult males were difficult to move as their weight would often break the harnesses used to transport the elephants, so they only moved females and young elephants.

It was not long before some of the transplanted young males became extremely unruly and violent, killing several rare white rhinos as well as a tourist and a professional hunter. The absence of adult male elephants seemed to be a major reason the young males were behaving so badly, as the socialization and guidance of the older males was seen as being critical to the young elephants' development. The park rangers built stronger harnesses for helicopter transport and moved a number of adult males to the new location. The problems with the young elephants soon went away as the old bulls quickly established boundaries and showed the young males what appropriate male elephant behavior looked like.

Dr. Horn theorized that some of the more violent gang activity, particularly that of some gangs terrorizing New York's Central Park several years ago, was similar to what had been observed in Africa among the elephants. Most of the young men involved in the violent gang behavior were without fathers and lacked the socializing influence of male adult role models and mentors. The leap Horn made from elephant behavior in Africa to gang behavior in Central Park may seem extreme, but I would not be one to dismiss the analogy based upon my coaching experience.

Fatherlessness leaves an emotional scar that is extremely hard to overcome. Robert Bly, author of the book *Iron John,* wrote, "Fatherless sons hang around older men like the homeless do around a soup kitchen. Like the homeless, they feel shame over their condition, and it is nameless, bitter, unexplainable shame."

I recall receiving a phone call from a father who had not seen his son, one of my players, for many years. He wanted to re-connect with his son who was blossoming as a football player and receiving national media attention. I notified the player that his dad had called and left his phone number. I thought the player would be pleased to hear from his father, but when I told him about the call his face darkened and he said words to the effect that "he left when I was a baby and the only reason he is calling now is because he read my name in the papers. He doesn't care about me." The pain in the player's voice was obvious, and it was easy to see he had been living with that pain for a long time and would likely carry it with him for the rest of his life. Unresolved issues with fathers (mothers too) often carry over into adulthood with devastating results.

The hurt I experienced over my father's absence during World War II was very minor compared to the grief many young people feel when a parent simply doesn't care enough to be involved in their life. I knew my dad loved me and was only involved in the war because he hoped it would make the world a better place for my brother and me to grow up in. Rejection and abandonment is another matter; it leaves a hole in the heart that is hard to heal.

I recently reviewed some letters written by high school graduates applying for scholarships. These young people had been part of the TeamMates Mentoring Program, had made significant improvement in their academic and personal development and were in the process of applying to colleges for admission and scholarships. A letter written by a young woman reflects the anguish most of the applicants expressed in one manner or another concerning lack of parental support. Her comments follow:

"Just imagine yourself in somebody else's shoes for a moment, and imagine being this child who was confused all through their childhood. This child was always around violence and always having to move from place to place. Being around someone most of your life who means so much to you, but then the next minute they are gone and you never know where they went. Thinking someone was somebody and they turned out to be somebody else. Not having control of what is going on around you. Having to adjust to something new once you just got used to being where you are. Having your life change so quickly. Not even having a chance to say goodbye. Finally realizing your real father and mother were never around. Could you do it? Do you remember when you were little and your parents told you to make a wish and blow out your candles? Most kids wished for a pony or a toy they wanted. My wish was for my parents to be home and be a family. Every birthday I wished for the same thing and to this day, I'm still waiting for that wish to come true. I always wondered what it would be like to have a mother and daughter's day and even a father and daughter's day. I always imagined what it would be like for my parents to wake me up in the morning so I could get ready to go to school. I even imagined that kiss and hug your parents gave you before you left. What it would be like to be on the court or on the track and be able to look up and see my family cheering for me in the stands. I've spent most of my life imagining this and wishing that. I have been that confused child whose life changed in the blink of an eye. For so long I've been stuck in the past trying to figure out why I was never happy and why nothing was ever going right."

While the letter above was written by a young woman who felt the absence of both parents, sometimes children caught in a tug of war between divorced parents experience a great deal of anguish as well. They are often caught between two parents competing for their attention and their loyalty.

One young person wrote:

"Some of the obstacles I have overcome would be growing up without a father figure in my life, because of how young I was I started to blame myself for what was happening. As I got older it hit me that it wasn't my fault and used my anger as motivation to graduate high school and attend college."

One of the major contributing factors to fatherlessness is the increasing out of wedlock birth rate. According to the United States Census Bureau, six percent of children were born outside of marriage in 1960. Today it is more than forty percent. I think it is safe to say that most of those children born out of wedlock grow up without fathers present in their lives and a great many never even know their fathers. Sometimes mothers also aren't committed to their children, and we find many grandparents raising their grandchildren.

Throughout our nation's history parents have wanted their children to have a better life than they did. That is still true with many today, but it does not appear to be as universal as it once was. Children need to be valued, nurtured and given a place of central importance if our culture is to remain strong.

It seems education level plays into the high outside of marriage birth rate. The Census Bureau points out that sixty five percent of high school dropouts have children while not married, whereas only eight percent of college graduates have births outside of marriage. The combination of lack of education and being a single parent leads to poverty in most cases, as seventy one percent of single parent families live in poverty, and many of those single parents lack sufficient education to earn a good income.

In asking young people who have been involved with Team-Mates what their greatest obstacle has been, many mention difficulties outside the family. Several experience problems with bullying. Anyone who has been exposed to verbal abuse by other students, ostracism, or even cyber bullying can relate to the hurt and confusion this causes. One young person expressed how painful this can be by writing the following: "In fifth and sixth grade I was a victim of bullying. I hated school, I would come home crying and not want to go back to school. It was the worst two years of my life. Every day at school I would be bullied, such as not being allowed to sit with the "popular" table. My dad got me involved in TeamMates. My mentor has changed my life. She has supported me and helped me deal with the bullies and tough challenges I faced. The bullying has made me a better person, and I made it a goal to help fight against bullying."

Unfortunately, many of our young people deal with bullying on a daily basis. In some instances the pain can become so extreme that it results in emotional illness or even suicide. It seems being able to express the hurt and anger engendered by bullying and talking through strategies to deal with it with a mentor is very therapeutic for many young people.

Mentors are also often very helpful in dealing with peer pressure to use drugs and alcohol, become sexually active, be involved with the wrong group of people and other destructive influences. Such negative influences have nothing to do with the family. Anyone exposed to today's youth culture is quickly convinced that navigating through childhood and adolescence is precarious business. Emerging on the other side of the process relatively healthy and unscathed usually involves good parenting, some luck, and often a good mentor.

Many children from intact, sometimes high income families don't escape the phenomenon of parental absence. With omnipresent technology and high pressure jobs many parents are consumed by their work to the degree that little time is left to be a parent. I am guilty as charged as I think back over the years when our children were growing up. My thirty six years in coaching were very time consuming. During the season we averaged more than eighty hours per week preparing for games, coaching on the field, dealing with player problems and concerns, recruiting, speaking and media obligations, etc.

The season lasted for six months, and then we launched into full time recruiting which was even more intense and time consuming. After spring football during March and April, recruiting during May and our football camps in June, we had about six weeks in which to live a normal life. Even that would sometimes be filled with demands of the job. I would try to make it up to my wife Nancy and our children during those few weeks, but I know it was never enough–and I know sometimes I let my passion for fishing interfere with even that small precious window of time.

I tried to approach coaching in as family friendly a manner as possible. We started our staff meetings at 7:00 am each day except Sunday, and we worked steadily reviewing films, preparing practice schedules and game plans until our players showed up for meetings at 2:00 pm. After meetings we went straight to practice and then, following practice, met as a staff until 10:30 pm on Sunday and Monday nights. We went home after practice on Tuesday, Wednesday and Thursday nights, whereas many coaching staffs met on those nights. I would bring films home and work until fairly late on those nights, but I still had dinner with my family and spent a little time with my three children and Nancy. Nancy commented that even though I was home those evenings and was physically present, I wasn't really there since my mind was on football

I spent Friday nights with the team as we prepared for the next day's game. We met on Saturday morning, played the game and then I had media duties afterward and graded the game film often until the wee hours. I gave the coaches Sunday mornings off so they could take their family to church if they so desired. We always attended church as a family, win or lose. After a loss people were usually decent, but they were a lot more friendly, even at church, when you won. Sprinkled throughout the week was a Sunday television show, a Monday quarterback club luncheon, a Tuesday night radio broadcast and an early Thursday morning breakfast in Omaha sixty miles away.

This sounds like a lot; however it was fairly humane considering what most other football coaching staffs were required to do. I recall talking to a young assistant coach at another school who had not seen his children in six weeks. He left his house at 6:00 am and got home after midnight seven days a week. His children were in bed when he left in the morning and back in bed before he got home at night. It is not unusual for coaches to sleep in their offices and not go home until the weekend. That particular young man couldn't stand the strain and left the coaching profession. Most stay with it if they can, but there is a heavy price to pay. The divorce rate is often high, and I'm sure that the children of coaches and their wives bear a difficult burden—my own included.

Such a schedule is very demanding, but unfortunately it is not limited to the coaching profession as many competitive, demanding jobs exact a similar price on families. With cell phones, laptops and iPads one can work nearly twenty four hours a day if sufficiently driven. The desire to accumulate money, TVs, automobiles, nicer homes, expensive vacations and job promotions has resulted in parents feeling the "need" to have two careers, two paychecks and often less time with children.

In the early 1960s, when I began my coaching career, I had never heard of cocaine or methamphetamine. I had heard of marijuana, but I didn't know anyone who had used it. As time went on the drug culture began to rear its ugly head and became a real concern for anyone interacting with young people on a daily basis.

In 1984, as soon as the technology became available, we began to test our players for drugs of all types, recreational and performance enhancing. We tested frequently, randomly, unannounced until right before the test was taken—in full view of our trainers so masking agents could not be used. The incidence of positive tests was small, less than two percent. Once a player tested positive he was given a professional evaluation and counseling and was then tested weekly on a random schedule. A second positive test resulted in suspension from the team for a period of time and a third positive test resulted in permanent dismissal from the program.

Some players who had tested positive responded well and became excellent players and role models, but most didn't. In examining their case histories we often found they had been involved with regular usage, usually marijuana, since junior high school and the addiction proved to be so strong that even with counseling and a desire to remain on the team, they would often have a third positive test and be dismissed.

I have been surprised at the legalization of marijuana. Data concerning marijuana use indicates that it inhibits short-term memory, negatively impacts motor skills, results in less personal drive and ambition and often leads to undisciplined behavior—all very bad qualities for a football player, a student, or an employee. Since the ingredient in marijuana which causes intoxication is fat soluble and is stored in fat cells in the brain, it remains in the body longer than alcohol and is easily detectable for several weeks. I am not championing alcohol usage, but alcohol is water soluble and leaves the system in a few hours. Marijuana has an impact on judgment, motor skills and memory for many days after usage and impairs the user over an extended period of time.

Most coaches and employers do not want someone on their team or payroll functioning at a subpar level, hence the drug testing for marijuana and other drugs. In my opinion, we are making a mistake by sending a signal to young people that marijuana is relatively harmless by legalizing it. Even though states which have legalized it have a twenty one year old age limit to purchase marijuana, it still sends a message that it is relatively harmless when it isn't. The marijuana sold today is much more potent than varieties sold many years ago, and it is often laced with other chemicals which can make the drug even more dangerous.

We treated alcohol as a drug as far as football team rules were concerned, so minor in possession of alcohol, driving under the influence, or underage consumption all qualified as positive drug tests. My best teams voted for total abstinence from alcohol and enforced it internally through team leadership. We saw almost zero usage of cocaine, heroin or methamphetamine. The abuse of pain killers and other prescription drugs became a concern after I left coaching in 1997, and by the time I became athletic director at Nebraska in 2007 those substance abuses were also on the radar.

The reason I am discussing drug abuse is that it doesn't just affect athletes. It has affected our whole culture and oftentimes the ones hurt most by substance abuse are our young people. Nothing has been as destructive to families and children as methamphetamine, a drug that was often used during World War II by enemy soldiers to create a feeling of invincibility as they went into battle. Japanese Kamikazi pilots were often high on methamphetamine as they departed on missions from which they had no possibility of returning.

Methamphetamine eventually arrived in the Unites States and was often manufactured in small home-made labs in rural areas so the odor and equipment used in its manufacture would not give its production away. Meth is so addictive (often with only one exposure) that the user often becomes incapable of caring about much of anything but the next hit. A Baylor University study showed that for every one percent increase in methamphetamine use foster care admissions rose by one and a half percent. During the 1980s and early 1990s foster care admissions due to parental addiction to meth rose from 280,000 to 408,000, a forty five percent increase.

When I served the Third Congressional District from 2000 until the end of 2005 I saw firsthand how destructive methamphetamine use was. My staff and I made drug awareness presentations at nearly every school in my district, which encompassed more than sixty counties and 64,000 square miles. The presentations were graphic. We showed students the key ingredients in the manufacture of meth: Drano, lithium batteries, iodine and pseudoephedrine. We showed pictures of the physical and mental toll meth took on people such as loss of hair, teeth, brain cells and the eventual price those using methamphetamine for extended periods pay, death. After nearly every school presentation young people would come to us and reveal the devastation meth had caused in their family or in the lives of someone they knew.

Losing a parent to addiction not only removes that parent from the child's life but also often leads to other problems. Research shows children of those who are addicted to alcohol or drugs are much more susceptible to becoming addicted as well. The cycle of addiction moves from one generation to the next unless something or someone intervenes to break the cycle.

One of the unfortunate outcomes of substance abuse and addiction is incarceration. I recently visited with a young prison inmate who agonizes over the effect his incarceration and separation from his little daughter is having on her. His main reason for wanting to be released from prison and live a productive life is so he can be a good father for his daughter. He knows life is hard for children of prisoners and that, despite their own difficult experience with a parent's imprisonment, a relatively high percentage of such children end up being incarcerated themselves.

The lack of support in the lives of so many of our young people, coupled with the challenging environments so many of them are forced to grow up in, has made this the most difficult time in our nation's history to be a young person. We are a privileged nation, yet in the midst of affluence we find many who are falling through the cracks. Mentoring is an excellent solution to many of the difficulties facing our young people today.

CHAPTER TWO
THE IMPACT OF TECHNOLOGY

I first noticed it in the 1980s. Players got on a team bus or airplane and donned a set of headphones. Prior to that time, there was always a good deal of conversation and banter among teammates. What once was a lively, interactive environment grew silent as everyone was listening to canned content coming through headphones. Next came cell phones, laptops, iPods and iPads. Players seated a few feet apart would text each other rather than carry on a conversation. We have developed a generation raised with technology, addicted to it, and, in some ways, imprisoned by it.

Most young people would rather play a video game than read a book, send a text message than carry on a conversation, tweet than be reflective. They are "connected" with others on Facebook, Instagram and SnapChat, yet they often lack meaningful relationships developed through personal, face to face interaction.

Dr. Tim Elmore, writing in his book *Generation iY,* records observations based upon research concerning young people born after 1990. He refers to this demographic group as "generation iY." This generation holds nearly half of the world's population and has grown up with technology of all types at its finger tips. It has access to all kinds of information in minutes which in the past would have taken days or weeks to acquire through library research, encyclopedias and newspaper files. They tend to be very well informed on topics in which they have an inter-

est. At the same time, Dr. Elmore points out, they are often overwhelmed and isolated by the amount of information coming at
them.

According to a 2007 American College Health Survey, 94
percent of college students feel overwhelmed by their lifestyle,
44 percent feel very depressed, and 10 percent considered suicide in the past year. Even though this survey involved college
students, I am sure the data reflects the feelings of a great many
young people who are not in college as well.

Our young people, according to the Kaiser Family Foundation, spend an average of seven and a half hours per day in front
of a screen. Through technology most young people spend large
amounts of time emailing, tweeting, texting and playing video
games, and even studying at times. They are accustomed to
things happening rapidly, volumes of information, much multi-
tasking and lots of noise. Slowing down, becoming well grounded, and knowing oneself is difficult to achieve in this environment.

Elmore points out this frenetic activity and sensory overload
often results in poor relationship and listening skills. Today's
young people also have less ability to empathize with others.
Technology is devoid of feeling. It is possible to destroy thousands of imaginary people in a video game without sensing that
there can be real pain involved in mayhem of this type when real
people are involved. It is one thing to break up with a girlfriend
online or to have an unpleasant exchange with a colleague
online, and quite another to do it face to face. Technology
removes much of the emotional wallop and interpersonal skill
that direct contact with another usually entails.

Young people, according to Elmore, are also often lacking in
tenacity. Their fast-paced world does not provide experience in
accomplishing tasks which are difficult, tedious and often take
weeks or months to accomplish. Television shows come to a

conclusion within a half hour to an hour, and movies end within two hours. They often want to start at the top when they take a job or join an athletic team. Many student athletes at the college level want to make an immediate impact. If things aren't quick and easy they often seek to transfer to another school–a place where their talents will be recognized and rewarded immediately. This mind set is very different than that of the athletes I coached early in my coaching career. Few thought they would play as freshman; most thought they would be second or third team in their second year and hoped to contribute a great deal in their third, fourth or fifth year. Very few transferred looking for greener pastures before they had even gotten adjusted to the team they started with.

All is not totally negative concerning the current generation, however. They truly want to make a contribution and are looking for ways to serve others. Unfortunately, though, this altruistic tendency also seeks quick resolution and gratification, not long-term commitment and sacrifice. We have found many college students sign up to be mentors, but often fail to show up consistently. We have had to be more selective in screening mentors of this age group. College students who are both interested and committed can be excellent mentors. They relate well to young mentees because of proximity in age and outlook. Finding college age mentors who possess staying power and patience has been difficult, however.

Many young people score well on measures such as IQ tests like ACT and SAT examinations, yet seem to possess relatively low amounts of Emotional Intelligence. Emotional Intelligence is hard to define. It has to do with being able to recognize one's own feelings and general emotional state and being able to read the same qualities in others. This skill results in an enhanced ability to communicate effectively with another person and be of help to that person. Emotional Intelligence is often very important in leadership positions, in counseling, parenting, mentoring and in sales positions.

Reading another person's emotional state and body language is not readily discerned through emails and text messages, rather it is best learned through interpersonal interaction. I recall during my years in Congress I asked staff members to talk directly with each other rather than to communicate by email whenever possible. Sometimes staff members would send email messages when seated in the next cubicle. Often emails came across as terse and sometimes abrasive when they were not intended to sound as they did. Voice inflection, a laugh or a smile, body language, often convey an entirely different message than what the recipient of an electronic message hears. It seemed personal contact in the office helped avert some hurt feelings and misunderstandings. Technology has led to diminished relational ability in many of our young people as they have had so little practice in face to face interaction. Mentoring builds relationship and communication skills. It offsets the isolation and the impersonal environment engendered by technology.

In the 1980s Dr. Benjaman Spock was seen by many to be the most authoritative voice concerning child rearing. He emphasized the importance of building self-esteem in children. The self-esteem movement gathered momentum and heavily influenced parents, teachers and those who wrote curricula in our nation's schools. Some schools eliminated dodge ball in physical education class for fear that those who were hit by the ball and eliminated early in the game would feel bad. Sometimes all young children running a race were given medals so no one would be a loser. Grading frequently became less strict and a "C" was no longer an average grade, rather it would be a "B" or even higher. More generous grading is now commonplace even in our colleges and universities. Parents were encouraged to offer praise to their children for even the most mediocre performance as long as the child made some kind of effort. It is small wonder that many young people become narcissistic as they internalize exaggerated estimates of their accomplishments and abilities and face little consequence for substandard performance.

The main difficulty with this effort to promote a positive self-image, no matter how badly the truth is distorted, is that young people often have trouble dealing with the inevitable failures and hard knocks life will deal them as they move into adulthood. If you have repeatedly been told you are the best, it is hard to be second or third string and sit on the bench or not immediately rise to the top of your company when you enter the workforce. Many coaches and employers have told me that our young people are talented, but also impatient; they don't want to work their way up. They want to start at or very near the top even though they are not ready for the responsibility. They have been sheltered to the degree it is hard for them to get back up when they get knocked down, to persevere through adversity, to be shaped and molded by failure and disappointment.

Nothing is quite as instructive as getting the tar beaten out of you in an athletic contest. When you win you think you have everything figured out and are resistant to change. When you suffer a bad loss, however, everything is open for discussion concerning what needs to change and what can be improved. Most growth occurs as a result of experiencing adversity, not abundance.

When I was coaching we had a particularly humbling experience during the 1990 season. We lost to Colorado in the middle of the season and then ended the season by losing badly to Oklahoma when our starting quarterback was hurt; we followed that loss with another decisive loss to Georgia Tech in the Citrus Bowl. Colorado and Georgia Tech were very good teams and ended up sharing the national championship that year, but the cold hard fact was that we weren't the team we should have been. So we re-evaluated every aspect of what we did, from recruiting, to off-season training, to offensive and defensive schemes, to relationships with players, to goal setting. From that examination of the program, changes were made that resulted in a period of excellence in which our five year record was sixty wins and three losses, with three national championships. Had we not experienced a difficult season in 1990 I doubt we would have made the changes that led to a considerable run of success.

Adversity can cause one to quit, to give up. It can also lead to blaming others or circumstance for one's difficulty. Or, it can result in a healthy examination of what led to the adversity and seeing it as an opportunity to learn and grow from a negative experience. Obviously quitting and blaming are not proactive, helpful responses. Seeing adversity as an opportunity to learn something, an opportunity to get better, can often result in great accomplishment.

So we have a paradox. As previously outlined, many children suffer from a lack of financial resources, of nurturing. On the other hand we have many children who are handicapped by excessive care from "helicopter" parents who hover around them and try to shield them from any kind of hurt or failure. Their self-esteem is to be protected and elevated at all costs. Even though both groups of children are handicapped—one by what they don't have, the other by what they have too much of, both are often overwhelmed by the sensory overload technology provides. Rich or poor, neglected or smothered by privilege, they nearly all have cell phones, television sets, iPods and all the other technology appendages which accompany modern life. Everything is coming at them very fast, sometimes from all angles, and the overload can be overwhelming.

THE MENTOR'S KEY FOCUS: UNCONDITIONAL LOVE

Not all children come from stable homes. Try as we might we have not been able to eradicate many of the negative outside influences impacting children such as substance abuse, gangs, bullying, pornography, and less than wholesome television, harmful rap lyrics and video games. So what do we do?

After giving much thought to the matter, it appears the best thing we can do is to provide each child who wants to have another caring adult in his or her life with a mentor. I would like to make it clear that many children coming from intact, stable families request a mentor. They simply sense at a certain juncture in their life they can benefit from the influence of an adult who has not been closely involved with them since infancy.

As one mentee wrote: "When I step back and look at everything my mentor has done for me, it makes me realize that young teenagers need somebody else who isn't their friend or family member to talk to. A mentor is somebody to talk to and it stays confidential." Another said this: "I know my mom loves me, but now I know that someone doesn't have to be family to care about you. My mentor is one of the best mentors I know, she is like a second mom to me, she has been with me through some of the toughest times in my life."

Nearly every parent has experienced a child coming home from school and expressing the importance of a "new" idea which was presented by a coach, a teacher, or a friend. The idea was something the parent had been urging the child to try for months, but it was only when an outside influence championed the idea that it gained relevance and was heard. The parent is often dumbfounded that this appears to be an entirely new thought to the young person, when the parent has urged the same idea many times previously. For some reason, having a person from outside the family encourage an activity legitimizes it.

Almost everyone who has enjoyed some level of exceptional achievement can point to at least one person who has been a major influence in his or her life at a critical juncture. Most successful people can name several such mentors from outside their families who have significantly impacted their lives. No matter how competent a parent is, there comes a time when others are seen as more wise and influential. Fortunately, this loss of status by the parent is usually not permanent and the young person comes to see his or her parents in a more favorable light when entering his twenties and thirties. An expert is usually someone who lives more than fifty miles away; familiarity often breeds contempt, particularly during the teen years.

So what is a mentor? A definition I found and like is the following: "a mentor is a coach, guide, tutor, facilitator, counselor, trusted advisor. A mentor is someone who is willing to spend time and expertise to guide the development of another person." The definition is a good one, but it is also a little sterile. Let me share my own perspective on what I believe mentoring is about.

The word love has many connotations. The Greeks recognized this long ago and used several different words to express the many facets of "love." Eros meant erotic love or romantic love; unfortunately our entertainment industry has emphasized erotic "love" to such a degree that our culture often thinks of the physical expression of love as the only dimension of the concept. The Greek word storge was most commonly used to describe a parent's love for a child and a child's love for a parent; it represented a strong natural family affection. Filia is love for a friend, a long-standing devotion to one who has shared interests and experiences.

Agape is unconditional, selfless love for another. It is willing the best, having unconditional positive regard, wanting the best outcome for another. Agape certainly can have a strong emotional component; however, it is possible to will the best for someone who is not your friend, who is unlovely. Jesus was referring to an agape kind of love when He was commanding people to "love your enemies." It is possible to will the best for another even though that person may be antagonistic. The neighbor who is unfriendly and doesn't speak can still be the recipient of your unconditional positive regard if you make up your mind that you will display a positive attitude toward that person no matter what he does. Agape is a form of love which is primarily an act of will, a supportive attitude toward another irrespective of circumstance. This type of love is crucial in mentoring.

So, the mentor wills the best and wants the best possible outcome for the young person being mentored. There will be days where things seem to click and both the mentor and mentee are in sync, and they share a strong bond. Then there will be those times when one or the other is having a bad day or is distracted, and the good feeling isn't there. However, if the mentee understands that the mentor is there to serve the mentee's best interests and truly cares about his or her well-being, the relationship will survive and thrive even though there will be occasional rough spots.

A mentee wrote the following about her experience: "When I started the program I was very young. When I met my mentor, I was dubious about her. I wasn't used to adults asking about my family and about me, in general. I can even say I was a bit cruel whenever she visited. I complained and whined about not wanting to talk. I didn't want to open up to a complete stranger. I felt as if she were prying on my life. I felt she was going to use me and then leave. Either way, she never failed visiting me. The summer before seventh grade I moved to Georgia and had to start all over. My mentor gave me her number and asked me to call whenever I wanted to. After a while I realized that I missed my mentor. I missed someone asking me how I was. It didn't matter how much it bothered me in the beginning, I wanted someone to care. I suddenly felt extremely ashamed and embarrassed that I had treated her so rudely, when she actually cared for me. It was with the same guilt, shame and sadness that I picked up the phone and dialed her number. It was probably one of the best things I have ever done. I later moved back to Omaha and my mentor visited me again. This time I appreciated it . . . I learned that I can't live my life doubting everyone . . . my mentor made me believe in myself. She told me I could do it when others said I couldn't. It's from those words of encouragement that I am here today." The young woman graduated from high school and is now attending college. She credits her mentor's unwavering love and faithfulness for what she has accomplished.

It is likely she wasn't properly prepared for her mentoring experience before she first met with her mentor. We find that by properly training the mentor and also explaining carefully what mentoring is about to the mentee we can avoid the rocky start this relationship had.

According to what this young woman writes, her mentor was given a rough time but consistently came to meet with her and continuously demonstrated her care for the mentee irrespective of how she was treated. Eventually the mentor's love broke through the shell of resistance and the mentee responded. This is something of an extreme case, but it is not unusual for a young person to be suspicious of a mentor's motives and mistrust the mentor initially. However, if the mentor continuously demonstrates love for the mentee, regardless of the response in return, the relationship will usually blossom.

A young man explained his relationship with his mentor in this way: "I met my mentor, five years ago, during my eighth grade year. At first I didn't know what to expect, but after several weeks I learned I could trust him. He was interested in getting to know me as a person, not as someone that needs to be controlled. The thing I really like about TeamMates is I can have a reliable person in my life I can fully trust with my problems. They actually care about the student, their future wellbeing, and how they do in school."

Sometimes a mentoring relationship develops without a time of doubting and testing the mentor's motives and commitment. For example, a mentee wrote the following about her mentor: "Being paired with a woman like (my mentor) has truly changed my life. She came into my life and gave me a voice. The thought of spending time with someone other than my friends or family members thrilled me. From the first time we talked outside of the classroom, I knew we were the perfect partners. (My mentor) has been an inspiration to me. I've looked up to her and she has taught me to follow my heart and my dreams. Without her, I know I wouldn't be the person I am today. . . . Having someone take your side, give you advice, and love you unconditionally is all anyone wants in their life."

The word "unconditional" seems to be especially important in a mentoring relationship. A mentor is sometimes better prepared to love unconditionally than a parent. As parents we have raised our children from infancy and have grown accustomed to directing and guiding them through toilet training, developing good manners, following directions, practicing the piano and a myriad of things we think they need to know and understand if they are our children and are to be good representatives of our families. In the process, children often are seen as extensions of the parent to the degree that it is difficult to objectively assess what is truly in the best interest of the child. Our own needs and our desire to have our children excel as "our" children often gets confused with what the child truly wants and needs.

For example, my son Mike really enjoyed skateboarding when he was eight or nine years old. He built a skateboard ramp in our driveway, and he and several neighborhood kids spent lots of time honing their skills and taking a few nasty falls on that ramp. We took a family vacation to Colorado, and the high point of the trip for Mike wasn't seeing the mountains or fishing in a pretty stream, rather it was visiting a skateboard park in Denver replete with all types of bowls, jumps and ramps.

My childhood had been devoted primarily to athletics. Whatever sport was in season was my chief pastime and passion. Because I was never able to get that devotion to athletic competition out of my system I became a coach. I thought Mike could have better spent his time playing football, basketball and baseball than going up and down that skateboard ramp in our driveway; I began to discourage his skateboarding career and pushed him toward various youth sports teams. Many of the young people in the skateboard culture had long hair and wore baggy pants which, in my eyes at that time, was a sure sign of a less than wholesome lifestyle.

So I began to push Mike toward Little League baseball, midget football and various youth basketball teams. Eventually the skateboard ramp came down, and he retired his skateboard in exchange for footballs, baseballs and basketballs. Although he wasn't quite as passionate about organized athletics as I had been, he went along with it and became a good athlete, playing high school football and basketball and starting for several years as a quarterback at the same college I had attended.

I think Mike benefited from his athletic experience, and I don't think it was unpleasant for him; however years later he expressed the fact that he resented the way I had pushed him away from skateboarding. I was interpreting what was best for

Mike through my own experience and was not really listening to what he wanted to do. My view of the world and what was important didn't coincide with the way he saw things, and I was not wise enough to see the difference. I would guess that he would have outgrown his skateboarding interest and would have gravitated toward team sports on his own, but the way I used my influence at that time was probably not in his best interest.

I'm sure a mentor would have seen Mike's situation more objectively and would have encouraged him to follow his heart in regard to his skateboarding. A mentor is removed from the situation enough to avoid interjecting his or her own feelings and experiences into the relationship. A mentor is often truly able to be more "unconditional" in offering love and support.

There are many stories of children being pushed into professions which are not of their choosing to please their parents and of young people marrying those who are acceptable to parents but are not the young person's choice. Many parents are able to remain sufficiently objective and wise to not unduly interfere in their children's lives when they become old enough to think for themselves, but it is often very difficult to back off at the appropriate time. We have been telling our children what to do since they were infants, and we often don't recognize when this needs to stop.

Another key word in mentoring is "commitment." We often think of love being a feeling; however, a major part of truly loving another person doesn't have to do with emotion nearly so much as being committed to that person. Commitment implies a steadfast dedication to the wellbeing of another through thick and thin, for better or for worse, in sickness or in health, no matter what the circumstance. Commitment is a decision and a promise. In reading some of the things mentees had to say in regard to their mentors, the theme of commitment keeps coming through. The mentor was consistently available and remained true to the mentee even during difficult times.

In doing research with the TeamMates Mentoring Program we have found that if the mentor meets with the mentee at least twenty four times in a school year of approximately thirty five weeks very positive outcomes occur. There will be vacations, times of illness, and occasions when there is bad weather, but if the mentor is faithful and meets regularly with the mentee, the mentee sees the relationship is stable, something that can be counted on.

When a person who has no obligation to serve another, is not a teacher, a parent, a grandparent, a preacher, a health professional, but is one who is willing to consistently show up and care for another unconditionally, it sends a message to the recipient of the type of love that they are significant, they have worth, they are valuable just for who they are. Receiving this type of love is transformative as the young person being mentored often begins to see himself in a new, more positive, light. Many of the negative feelings and perceptions all of us have internalized at one time or another begin to be dispelled by this type of unconditional love expressed through a commitment of time, attention and acceptance.

We also have found if a mentor enters a relationship with a young person with the promise of a long term commitment to that mentee, and the mentor doesn't follow through, great damage can be done. Therefore, in our training of new mentors we emphasize the importance of consistency, of following through on promises, of being on time. We want the mentee to understand the mentor is someone whom they can trust, someone who will be a constant in their lives even when there may be other circumstances which are unstable and unreliable.

Our average length of match is thirty six months, compared to a national average length of match of less than one year. This thirty six month average includes new matches. Since we are adding more than one thousand mentor-mentee matches per year, averaging in the new matches pulls the average match length down. Ideally we would like our matches to begin in elementary school and persist through high school graduation. Many of our matches last for eight or nine years and even stay in contact long after the young person leaves school. We ask for a commitment of a minimum of one year. If the mentor moves or can no longer continue mentoring, we try to find another mentor as soon as possible.

A mentor's unconditional love is of great importance in the mentoring relationship. Essentially the mentor asks the young person to share their hopes and dreams, those things which are of greatest importance to them. Then the mentor does the best he or she can to assist the mentee in realizing those dreams. The mentor accepts the mentee just as he is and becomes an advocate for the mentee. The mentor does not try to "fix" the mentee but rather show his love and support by consistently being present and nurturing the relationship.

A young woman described the impact unconditional love can have when she wrote this: "Before (my mentor), I was a very shy person and not very experienced in talking to an older adult like her. She helped me break out of my comfort zone and talk to her and other people without fear. I can tell her anything and love her as if she was another grandma to me. The conversation we engage in is different from any conversation with my peers, teachers, or family. She is an older adult I treat with a lot of respect and talk to differently. Maybe because I do not see her every day or because she is not a relative, I can talk to her in a way that brings about a more mature person in myself. Having her as a mentor has helped me see that we have only so much time to live and helping others is the best way to live. She does not have to come meet me every week, but she does anyway because she knows I enjoy talking with her. I plan on keeping in touch with her as I move forward with my life after high school because she has had such an impact on shaping me into the person I am today."

CHAPTER FOUR

STRENGTHS AND AFFIRMATION

Affirmation is very powerful. Used as a verb, affirmation may be defined as "a declaration that something is true." Used as a noun, affirmation means "emotional support or encouragement." We often carry perceptions about ourselves which have been implanted in our psyches when we were very young. A child who has been told that he or she is intelligent will often carry that perception throughout his or her lifetime. Someone who worked extensively in the prison population once noted a very common tattoo among prisoners was "born to lose." In all likelihood the prisoners bearing that tattoo had been told many times as children they would not do well, that they were "losers." Convinced of the accuracy of the "loser" label, many lived out their lives in such a way that the tattoo they wore was prophetic.

I saw the importance of affirmation during my years in coaching. If we told a player we believed in him, and he would one day be an outstanding player if he continued to work hard, we would often see a considerable improvement in performance and demeanor. Sometimes a player, energized by words of affirmation would grow into the player he had no idea he was capable of becoming. We tried not to discourage players, but a look of disgust or a negative comment would often trigger self-doubt and a decline in performance. Even large, strong football players have fragile egos and can be impacted significantly by what coaches think of them.

Lou Holtz, the former coach and current television sportscaster, once visited our practices and sat in our meetings with players. Lou visited while he was the head football coach at Arkansas. Before he left he told me the thing which most impressed him about his visit to Nebraska was how positive our coaches were; he had never observed that amount of positive feedback in the coaching world before. Often coaches see "coaching" as finding fault, criticizing. We thought it was important to catch a player doing something right and to praise and reinforce the desired action rather than constantly criticizing. If a player made a mistake, it was important to not personally attack him by questioning his intelligence, courage or commitment, but rather to explain clearly what he had done wrong and what we wanted him to do the next time in a way that was supportive and reflected confidence in his ability to get it right.

Often when some of our freshmen arrived on campus we could see they were a long way from being major college football players, and once in a while we would hear a coach say that a young man would "never play here." That type of labeling was discouraged. We continually saw young people make tremendous improvement as they matured, worked in the weight room and perfected their skills. Many of those who were thought to be unlikely to ever play became some of our best players in their third or fourth years.

Henry Ford once said "whether you think you can or think you can't–you are right." Those who think they can are usually people who have had parents, a teacher, a coach or a mentor who has given them the idea they can achieve great things. Those who think they can't are often people who have received negative messages about their abilities at critical junctures in their lives, usually when they are quite young.

Affirmation, statements such as "I believe in you," "I know you can do it," "You have unusual talent," and "You always come through in a tight situation" are powerful, but they must be rooted in reality. To tell someone who has little or no musical talent that they will one day become a great concert pianist is not only inaccurate, it is also cruel. It builds up a false expectation which will almost certainly be dashed when the person one day realizes she will never achieve the success which she had been led to believe she would.

All of us have talents, things that we do better than other things. Yet, surprisingly, many people aren't aware of their talents. Talents, or strengths, often come easily to us. They are natural and are often taken for granted, so we don't really identify them as strengths. We assume that nearly everyone else can do the same thing, has the same strengths, yet each person is unique and has special gifts.

During my years in graduate school at the University of Nebraska in the early 1960s I came in contact with a professor who was starting to think about the importance of strengths. Dr. Don Clifton taught in the Educational Psychology Department, and his work deviated markedly from the standard areas of psychological study at that time. Much research was devoted to the study of animals during that period, mostly mice and rats, but sometimes chimpanzees, dogs and other animals. It was believed that if we could begin to understand why a rat would turn right or left in a maze, or why a mouse would hit a lever a certain number of times in order to get a pellet of food, or why a monkey would perform a task to get a banana then we could eventually move up the phylogenetic scale in our research and be able to determine what made human beings tick.

If psychologists weren't studying animals, most of the research had to do with the study of abnormal behavior and mental illness in people. Don Clifton quoted psychologist Martin Seligman who said, "Psychology is half-baked, literally half-baked. We have baked the part about mental illness. We have baked the part about repair and damage. But the other side is unbaked. The side of strengths, the side of what we are good at, the side . . . of what makes life worth living."

Don Clifton was fascinated by exceptional performance and by the unique talents and strengths of people. In his book *Now Discover Your Strengths* he set forth two primary premises: One being that each person's talents are unique and enduring, and another being each person's greatest room for growth is in the area of his greatest strength. He stated "our research into human strengths does not support the extreme, and extremely misleading, assertion that you can play any role you set your mind to, but it does lead us to this truth: whatever you set your mind to, you will be most successful when you craft the role you play to your signature talents most of the time." He added that "Rapid learning, yearning to engage in a task or activity again, being absorbed in an activity to the point where one loses track of time, deriving satisfaction from the activity completion, is a sign that strengths are in play."

One young mentee said this: "I have always dreamed of standing in front of thousands of people and singing my heart out because that's what I love doing." She is obviously referring to an area of strength, and I would imagine that she has an excellent chance of achieving success as a singer. This is what she is passionate about and what she dreams about doing.

A young man wrote: "I plan on majoring in psychology in college. The reason I chose psychology is because of my experience with TeamMates. Meeting with my mentor and being able to talk about anything and everything benefited me tremendously. I want to give someone that type of encouragement and unconditional support. I want to be able to help people conquer their fears and difficulties. After college, I plan on attending medical school to become a psychiatrist." This young man obviously has the strength of empathy, which his mentor modeled for him and encouraged in him. He saw how his mentor's ability to listen empathetically benefited him and desires to do the same for others.

We have come to believe that identifying the strengths of young people and then affirming those strengths accomplishes several things:

1. Most people are not aware of their strengths. Discovering the fact that they have areas of unique talent is exciting to them.
2. Gallup research has shown that discovering and exploring the strengths of a young person through the mentoring experience causes the mentee to look forward to seeing the mentor to an even greater degree than before.
3. Research has also shown that discovering one's strengths leads to an increased level of hope in the mentee. Knowing that one has special talents makes a young person more hopeful about the future and about their ability to accomplish great things with their life.

In speaking with Allyson Horne, a specialist in training mentors in the use of strengths in the TeamMates Mentoring Program, I found it is important to have the mentors take the Gallup Strengths Finders instrument before the mentee takes the survey. We find many mentors are just like their mentees in that they usually aren't aware of their strengths and are not even aware they have special qualities which might be categorized as "strengths."

By taking the index before the mentee takes it, the mentor gains a better perspective of what his strengths are and how those strengths may play into how he sees and relates to his mentee. For example, one who is particularly strong in the "Relator" theme enjoys close relationships and likes working with others. On the other hand, a mentor who scores high in the "Analytical" theme will look for reasons behind behavior, may be more detached and will not develop strong relationships quickly.

The Relator may have to guard against developing too close a relationship too quickly, while the Analytical person may have to guard against being too reserved and remote while considering various nuances of the mentoring relationship.

A mentor whose number one strength is "Command," an ability to take control of situations and make decisions, may need to be sensitive to not being too authoritarian if matched with a young person who possesses a strong "Deliberative" theme. A Deliberative theme would indicate a tendency to be very cautious and thoughtful in making decisions. One whose strength is Command may become impatient with a Deliberative child who is slow to arrive at a course of action.

By identifying one's own strengths as a mentor and by seeing the mentee's strengths as well, a mentor can relate more effectively. It is particularly important for the mentor to point out and affirm a strength when it is displayed in some aspect of the young person's behavior. For example, a mentee who is high in the Achiever strength index will often accomplish something academically which is out of the ordinary for that child. This might be something such as obtaining an "A" in algebra when "C" work had been the norm. This accomplishment may have started with the student establishing a goal of getting an "A" and then putting in extra study time to achieve the grade. The mentor can then point out that Achievement is a major strength for the young person, and the process which led to the "A" is an example of that theme being a major part of who that mentee is and how this strength will be important going forward.

A child who has a "Futuristic" theme is one who is visionary and inspired by future possibilities. Such a child may embark on a project which requires the ability to see over the horizon and anticipate a future need in the community, maybe a better way to recycle waste at the school, or improvements in living arrangements for an aging population. It is important to not dismiss such plans as too impractical, as most innovative ideas which have had great value were once thought to be of no use. A visionary person may have many trials and failures but ultimately may come up with a great idea which is unique and will benefit many.

Gallup lists 34 major themes, or strengths. In taking strengths assessments older students are informed of their five major themes; younger children, taking a different index, are provided three. A younger child has often not developed enough self-awareness to clearly differentiate among a larger number of themes. We find that when a child is made aware of his strengths and thinks about how those strengths can be utilized, the future often appears brighter and possibilities open up which at one time appeared to be beyond reach. Hope is a powerful thing.

CHAPTER FIVE

MY GRANDFATHER'S STORY

We tend to see the future through the lens of past experience. If a young person has grown up in a home where education is valued and both parents and most relatives have attended college, she will usually assume a college education is part of her future and will plan accordingly. The question is not "if" I will go to college, but rather "where" will I go to college? A young person who has grown up in a home where no one has attended college and higher education has never been discussed will likely develop an expectation that college is not an option and will plan for a future which does not include the prospect of higher education.

A mentor can often provide a fresh perspective concerning what the future might hold for a young person. This perspective quite often involves strengths the mentor has observed in the young person being mentored.

When I speak to groups about the importance of mentoring I often reference a story about my grandfather and how the person who mentored him saw a strength my grandfather possessed and how that strength was very important in planning his future.

I discovered the story about my grandfather's mentor in a roundabout way. My father always stated his name as Charles C. Osborne on his stationery and any formal documents. I asked him what the "C' stood for, but he would never tell me, which was puzzling. After my father passed away I had a conversation with my father's brother, Howard Osborne, and the matter of the middle initial came up. Howard said the initial stood for the name Currens, which my dad had never liked, hence his reluctance to reveal the name behind the initial. Howard went on to explain that the Reverend James Currens had been a very important figure in my grandfather Tom Osborne's life, and he had given his oldest son, my father, the name "Currens" as his middle name.

Curious about Currens, I did some investigating and found he had been a Sabbath School missionary who was appointed by the Presbyterian Board of Home Missions to ride a circuit in eastern Wyoming, western South Dakota and western Nebraska to establish Presbyterian churches and schools throughout the region. His appointment began in the early 1890s, a time when the area was being settled by farmers who were taking advantage of the Homestead Act, which provided one hundred and sixty acres of free land to settlers who would live on the land for a year and establish residency.

Currens had the reputation of being extremely hard-working and diligent in performing his duties. He either rode horseback or drove a horse-drawn cart for countless miles, year round across a vast lonely area in which roads were often no more than trails and were treacherous in bad weather. Currens established thirty four churches, which often began with no more than a tent and two or three families in a small community. Most of those churches are still in existence today.

My grandfather Osborne was born in Illinois and moved to Nebraska in 1887 when his family came west to homestead near the small community of Bayard. His father, my great-grandfather, had fought in the Civil War on the Union side and saw an opportunity to better his family's lot by acquiring some land at no cost. In order to gain title to the land one had to live on the land long enough to establish residency; this was usually a year.

There were four children in the family, and I understand my great grandfather had a drinking problem, so there were likely times of considerable hardship. The land he homesteaded was not high quality land such as was common in Illinois, rather it was somewhat sandy and the average rainfall was less than half the amount Illinois would receive. The land overlooked the North Platte River Valley and had a view of Chimney Rock, a well-known landmark for the early settlers traveling the Oregon Trail as they headed west in search of land and gold. I doubt the view compensated for the difficult circumstances in which my grandfather was raised as his family sought to eke out a living in an unsettled region of the country on marginal land in a semi-arid climate.

My grandfather was listed as the only seventh grade student at "old 96" as the school in Bayard was known. The year was 1892, and it must have been a year or two earlier that Currens' travels intersected with my grandfather's life. Currens heard my grandfather give a talk at a school or a church event and was quite impressed. He told my grandfather he had unusual speaking ability for such a young person and he could envision him one day being an outstanding preacher. Each time Currens' travels would take him in the vicinity of Bayard he would spend time visiting with my grandfather, affirming his gift for public speaking and providing a vision of how that gift might be used in the ministry.

There were obstacles to realizing this vision, however. Bayard, like most small towns of that day in Nebraska, had a school which offered only seven or eight grades. The closest high school was in Crawford, Nebraska, located ninety miles to the northwest. Currens informed my grandfather that in order to become a preacher he would need to further his education by not only graduating from high school but also attending college before attending seminary. Having completed the seventh and

highest grade Bayard had to offer, with Currens' encouragement, my grandfather enrolled in Crawford Normal in December of 1892 with virtually no financial support. He got a job in a
local grocery store and was able to pay for his room and board
and his schooling. Money must have been scarce, however, for
when the school year ended in May he had only enough money
to ride the train the forty miles from Crawford to Alliance. With
no funds remaining he walked the remaining fifty miles home to
Bayard. He would have been about twelve or thirteen years old
at the time.

With Currens' encouragement he began to do some speaking at Sunday School events and eventually began to conduct
Sunday services at Camp Clarke, a trading post located a few
miles east of Bayard along the Platte River. He worked at the
trading post for a time, where his interaction with German, Rus-
sian and Hispanic immigrants as well as Ogallala Sioux Native
Americans enabled him to speak five languages fluently.

Upon graduating from Crawford Normal, Currens encouraged him to attend Hastings College, a small Presbyterian college located in Hastings, Nebraska. My grandfather rode a stage-
coach from Bayard to Alliance and then caught a train bound for
Hastings three hundred miles to the east, arriving with $4 left in
his pocket. He got a job taking care of a horse and a cow to pay
for his room and board.

Not many people living in Western Nebraska at that time
had a high school education, and almost no one went to college.
As a matter of fact, few people in the entire country attended
college, save for a small number from wealthy families and a few
others who wanted to go into the ministry. Most colleges and
universities of that time existed for the primary purpose of training people for the ministry.

During his time at Hastings College my grandfather had to
take two years off to earn enough money to finish school. He

returned to Bayard and worked as a school teacher, a railroader, a sheepherder and an irrigation ditch rider.

During his time working as a sheepherder he was bitten by a rattlesnake. At the time it was believed the best cure for a snake bite was a good slug of whiskey. However, probably because of his experience with his father's drinking, my grandfather had taken a vow to never drink alcohol. He refused the whiskey even though it was the best known "cure." Fortunately he survived the snake bite. The episode, however, points to the fact that he took his vow seriously, even if honoring the vow might cost him his life. He eventually saved enough money to return to Hastings.

During his two year absence from college he decided to acquire some land through the Homestead Act, as his parents had done. He lived on the land for a period of time and, thinking he had met the requirements for ownership, submitted his claim to the North Platte claims office. He returned to school assuming he now owned a piece of property.

He graduated from Hastings College in the spring of 1901, part of a senior class consisting of only four people. One of those four students was Julia Jones, daughter of a carriage retailer in Hastings. He was also captain of his football team in his senior year. Football was a particularly rough sport in those early years, with many severe injuries and deaths. It was so rough that President Teddy Roosevelt called a meeting in Washington four years later with the intended purpose of abolishing the game.

My grandfather married Julia Jones and enrolled in a seminary located in Bellevue, Nebraska, close to Omaha. After completing his seminary studies he accepted a pastorate at the Presbyterian Church in Wayne, Nebraska, a small town in the northeastern part of the state. It was during this time he found out that he was not a proud landowner. His homestead application had been turned down.

Since he was committed to his pastorate in Wayne, it was determined that someone needed to live on the land for another year, but it wouldn't be my grandfather because of his preaching contract in Wayne. Therefore, my grandmother traveled several hundred miles west and lived on the land to satisfy terms of the Homestead Act. My grandmother spent the year living on the land in a sod house with her infant daughter, Emily. She survived a major blizzard in isolated surroundings during that year and endured a great deal of hardship. She had no running water, indoor plumbing or close neighbors. Despite all she went through, the homestead application was turned down again by an official in North Platte. It turned out that the official was illiterate, so he turned everyone's homestead application down since he didn't know how to read the papers. After two attempts to "prove up" on the land my grandparents still had no title.

My grandfather eventually came west and was able to establish residence on the land and pastor several churches in Western Nebraska. He served churches in Alliance, Scottsbluff and Bayard. He had five children, Emily, Charles (my father), Clifford, Howard and John, all of whom graduated from Hastings College during the Great Depression. Charles, Howard and Clifford were all football players at Hastings College. Emily was a talented musician, my father became a businessman in Hastings, Clifford was a professor and a professional singer, Howard became a preacher and John, following a brief stint as a teacher, was killed in a training crash while serving in the Air Force during WWII.

My grandfather served two terms in the Nebraska State Legislature. One of his opponents for the Legislature was A. B. Wood, publisher of the Gering Courier newspaper. Mr. Wood wrote the following to my grandfather when it became apparent that my grandfather would win the election: "I am very sure there has been nothing in this campaign of a personal character, certainly nothing from me, and I have heard of no unkind words coming from you, hence I can vouchsafe my best wishes to you without reservation." If only present day politics were of a similar nature.

In his sixties, my grandfather had problems with his voice and had to quit preaching. He and my grandmother went back to their old homestead and were raising turkeys when my grandfather was struck by lightning while watering the turkeys from a pump. The year was 1945. The war was winding down, but my dad was still overseas.

Most of the early settlers of the area wanted the "reverener" to officiate at their funerals. Many of those folks had never darkened the door of a church but had sufficient respect for my grandfather to want him to usher them out of this world and into the next.

And so, my grandfather had a good life. It was altered considerably by the vision and influence his mentor Currens provided. Without Currens, I doubt my grandfather would have had any thought of going to college or even high school. I doubt he would have considered going into the ministry. I am sure he would not have met the woman he married. I am certain he would have been a different husband and father. I am sure he was talented enough that he would have led a productive life in some capacity, but I doubt he would have impacted anywhere near the number of people he influenced throughout his lifetime. His brothers and sisters were good people and lived good lives but none had the education to have the impact my grandfather had. Vision makes a difference, and the vision Currens provided my grandfather made a huge difference.

Further, Currens' influence on my grandfather had a ripple effect; his children were raised with the understanding that a college education was something which was expected and that living a life of service to others was required. In return, those children, educated through the difficult times of the Dust Bowl and the Great Depression of the 1930s, raised their children with similar expectations—and those grandchildren raised their children in much the same way with a similar world view. As one of those grandchildren I realize I owe a great debt to Currens, a man I never met but who made a great impact on our family, and on me.

I can remember being in my grandfather's presence only two or three times, as the war came along and I lived with my maternal grandparents three hundred miles away. However, I always looked up to him as an educated and accomplished man I admired and aspired to be like. Unfortunately I was only eight when he was killed by the lightning bolt, and I never got to see him again.

As I was growing up I assumed he was in heaven and could see every move I made. I was concerned I might not live up to his legacy, and I might let him down. That ripple effect which a mentor like Currens triggered goes on for many generations and impacts many people; it is not just a one-to-one, one-time thing which quickly fades and dies.

I can see the impact Currens had on my family through four generations. Through his influence my father, myself, my children and now my grandchildren have been expected to complete a college education, to be people of faith and to have certain values.

I could have related many stories concerning mentors who have had a dramatic influence on the young people they mentored. Those stories are just as remarkable as my grandfather's story and are much more current. The reason I chose to relate the story concerning Currens and my grandfather is that it happened more than one hundred years ago and illustrates the multi-generational impact a mentor can make. A mentor can, by influencing one life for the better, have a significant impact on dozens, and sometimes hundreds, of other people over many years.

I spend much of my time recruiting mentors. One of the things I stress when doing so is to point out that they, by helping one person live a better and more productive life, will be impacting not just one life but many more. The person the mentee marries, the children and grandchildren resulting from that marriage, the people who interact with that person in the workplace, the people who benefit from the mentored person's desire to serve and help others as a result of what they have been given by their mentor, will ripple on in the lives of countless people through many generations.

An example of the power of mentoring and the multi-generational effect which lives on in perpetuity is the influence Jesus had on the lives of twelve rather ordinary men He mentored over a three year period. Eleven of the twelve were impacted by this experience in such a way they devoted their lives to mentoring others, who then mentored others and the process continued in such a way that, through multiplication over two thousand years, there are more than two billion followers of a humble carpenter who mentored and impacted the lives of a small number of very common men.

CHAPTER SIX

THE IMPORTANCE OF MEANING & SERVICE

Victor Frankl, in his classic book, *Man's Search For Meaning*, chronicled his reflections on the meaning of life he gathered from his experiences as a Jewish prisoner of the Nazis during World War II. Frankl was trained as a psychiatrist, and during his years of enduring unspeakable suffering and brutality, which included the execution of his wife and his parents, he was still able to observe his reactions and those of his fellow prisoners with detachment and professional insight. He saw that there could be meaning and purpose even in the desperation and hopelessness of Auschwitz.

He noted that even though death in a gas chamber or by a firing squad might be imminent, some prisoners maintained a sense of dignity and displayed concern for their fellow prisoners. Others gave in to despair or a brutish survival instinct in which they lost all semblance of human compassion and concern for others. He wrote:

"We who lived in concentration camps can remember the men who walked through the huts comforting others, giving away their last piece of bread. They may have been few in number, but they offer sufficient proof that everything can be taken from a man but one thing: the last of the human freedoms–to choose one's attitude in any given set of circumstances, to choose one's own way."

He went on to say:

".... In the final analysis it becomes clear that the sort of person the prisoner became was the result of an inner decision and not the result of camp influences alone. Fundamentally, therefore, any man can, even under such circumstances, decide what shall become of him—mentally and spiritually. He may retain his human dignity even in a concentration camp."

A study done by Baumeister, Vohs, Aaker and Garbinsky published in the *Journal of Positive Psychology* examined the subject of perceived happiness and meaning in the lives of 397 subjects. The study found there was a small correlation between happiness and meaningfulness, but there were also major differences. The researchers found happiness is mostly tied to present feelings, living in the moment, having basic needs met and receiving benefits from others. Having enough money to purchase life's comforts was related to happiness but had little relation to purpose and meaning.

Meaning was related to dedicating oneself to serving others or dedication to a cause that transcended self rather than receiving or taking from others. In other words, being happy relates to taking and receiving, while meaning and purpose is related to giving and spending oneself on behalf of others. Having meaning and purpose in one's life tends to be enduring, while happiness is often fleeting and dependent upon feelings of satisfaction with present circumstances. Being "happy" and having a meaningful life are not necessarily congruent. Serving and sacrificing for others may actually lead to increased tension and unhappiness. Devotion to family members and friends provides meaning but also often involves a certain amount of stress and heartache as we see those we care about go through difficult times. Being a parent is often stressful and devoid of "happiness," yet it is often the most meaningful experience a person can have.

Many Americans report an absence of meaning and purpose in their lives; they may be "happy" because they have most of their immediate needs satisfied, but they see no significance in their existence. I recently had a conversation with a man who had obviously done well in the business world. I gathered he was relatively well off financially. He told me that even though he was considered to be "successful," he was lacking meaning and purpose in his life. He decided being a mentor would add a dimension of meaning which seemed to be lacking. I hope he followed through on his promise to mentor; I think he will find it to be very rewarding.

Frankl cited a study done by Johns Hopkins University involving 7948 students from across the United States in which seventy eight percent said that finding purpose and meaning in their lives was of primary importance. Despite the fact that so many people believe having meaning and purpose in their lives is of great importance, far too few find it. Young people often report they are "bored." Retirees think that a life free of job responsibilities in which they can enjoy themselves in an endless round of pleasurable activities often find retirement wasn't what they thought it would be. They begin to realize the responsibility which their jobs imposed upon them also gave them a sense of purpose without which they began to experience a vacuum, a sense of meaninglessness. Deprived of a purpose for living, many retirees don't live the long happy retirement which they had envisioned, rather they often experience the many maladies of advancing age and succumb to premature deaths.

During his years in Auschwitz, Frankl noticed those who had a sense of meaning and purpose in their lives seemed to be able to survive unspeakable brutality and hardship while those who lacked purpose, something to live for, often simply lost the will to live and passed away relatively quickly. Therefore he postulated that having a sense of purpose, seeing an ultimate meaning to one's existence, was nearly as important as having the basic requirements to sustain life: food, air and water.

So what provides meaning and purpose? Frankl thought one

of the primary ways in which meaning could be found would come from loving another person. He wrote: "love is the only way to grasp another human being in the innermost core of his personality. No one can become fully aware of the very essence of another human being unless he loves him. By his love he is enabled to see the essential traits and features of the beloved person; and even more, by his love, the loving person enables the beloved person to actualize these potentialities. By making him aware of what he can be and of what he should become, he makes those potentialities come true."

Frankl is describing very well what a mentor does in the mentoring relationship. By loving the mentee unconditionally, by determining strengths, and by providing affirmation, the mentor strives to enable the mentee to become that which he is capable of becoming. And the interesting thing is that the mentee, the one being helped, also benefits the mentor in a significant way, by helping the mentor find purpose and meaning in his own life.

When we dedicate ourselves to the well-being of another, someone who on the surface of things can do nothing for us in return, we also develop a deeper sense of purpose to our existence. Mentoring will entail times of "happiness" in which we experience moments of enjoyment in the company of the one we are mentoring, however, it will also entail times of stress and sorrow as we share in the struggles and disappointments in the life of the one being mentored. The most important thing to understand, however, is that despite the ups and downs of any important relationship, it will nearly always result in a greater sense of meaning and purpose.

Rick Warren, in his book *The Purpose Driven Life: What On Earth Am I Here For?*, said this: "Time is your most precious gift because you only have a set amount of it. You can make more money, but you can't make more time. When you give someone your time, you are giving them a portion of your life that you'll never get back. That is why the greatest gift you can give someone is your time. It is not enough to just say relationships are important; we must prove it by investing time in them. Words alone are worthless."

Giving someone your time is your most precious gift indeed. Giving time to someone also results in gaining something in return—a greater sense of meaning and purpose in one's life. Dr. Rachel Reman, in her book *My Grandfather's Blessings* says this about meaning. "Meaning is a form of strength. It has the power to transform experience, to open the most difficult of work to the dimension of joy and even gratitude. Meaning is the language of the soul. Few works of service can endure unless they are sustained by a lived sense of their meaning and purpose." Even though mentors do not always clearly articulate that mentoring provides them with a sense of purpose and meaning, I think most of them sense the added dimension which mentoring gives their lives is that of meaning and purpose.

In asking a number of mentors who had mentored for several years what they gained from the mentoring experience I received roughly five different categories of responses, which are as follows:

1. **Mentors really enjoy seeing the mentee mature and grow.** One mentor wrote, "My first mentee was a shy young man whose parents spoke only Spanish. He had three younger brothers. Today he is a senior at UNL, a good student with a double major in Spanish and Education, working on an ESL and coaching endorsement . . . His next oldest brother is a sophomore at Creighton, with a full tuition scholarship. I see his two youngest brothers being recognized as students of the month. I believe my mentees' example gave the rest of the family motivation to work hard and be successful." This mentor most likely had a powerful impact not

only on the young man he mentored, but on three younger brothers as well, as they saw the importance of academic commitment in their older brother's life and the direction it was taking him. Realizing the difference one can make in another person's life, and, in turn impacting many others is a very gratifying experience.

Another said, "My mentee has gone from missing several days of school to attending almost every day and made it on the honor roll. When I met her she didn't even know what the honor roll was. I showed her that most of the kids on the honor roll were also on the perfect attendance list. She told me all the kids on that list were smart. I let her know that she was smart too and explained the importance of attendance. She has made great strides and I am so proud of what she has accomplished."

Still another mentor commented, "In my nine years of mentoring the same child, I have grown to love and respect her as part of my family. I've watched her grow into a very talented, determined and awesome adult. She has gone from wanting to be a police woman to wanting to make a career out of professional skate boarding to now becoming a talented musician. Her dreams are coming true, and I couldn't be happier. She has her feet on the ground and is a loving, caring young lady."

Finally this, "Without a doubt, seeing your mentee succeed, even at the small things, is the most rewarding. For my first mentee, high school graduation was the highlight of our mentoring relationship. Since graduation I've been able to continue our relationship and see him transition to a good job. Knowing my mentee has a positive path for his life is very satisfying." Quite often mentoring results in a life-long relationship in which the mentor is able to see the positive effects of mentoring play out over many years.

2. Mentors often report that in the process of mentoring they find they become better parents. One mentor said, "The time spent with her has made me more appreciative of my own three girls and my husband. I have learned that kids really do appreciate someone just being there for them no matter what the situation. I think that's something we forget when dealing with our own children. .... If I didn't work every day I would take on more visits as I do think there are lots of kids who need someone who will just listen and be there for them."

One mentor was quite eloquent in explaining what his mentoring relationship had done in his life. "I believe mentoring has helped me to be a better listener, a better friend, a better leader, and a better father. My first goal as a mentor was to engage my mentee in our relationship. That process took a lot of time—and I'm not normally a patient person. I've applied that lesson to so many areas of my life, because my patience paid off. We are very close now and enjoy an authentic relationship based on truly knowing and respecting one another. My next lesson was to learn how to listen more and talk/act less. This is a lesson that has impacted every area of my life. At first, it wasn't too difficult to keep my mouth shut when my mentee told me some of the mistakes he made. I didn't have a vested interest. So I could easily ask questions like, 'so how did that work out for you?' In so doing he was able to explore the ramifications of his decision making without feeling judged. Instead, he felt supported. The results were amazing, and I found myself wondering why I didn't use the same approach with my own kids. Lastly, I've never been one to enjoy playing games. However, with my mentee it was the primary way we connected. Keeping busy and focused on the game allowed us to talk and share feelings in a safe way. Eventually, however, we no longer needed the games. Now we just sit and talk. It's amazing. I realized playing games isn't about me–it's about the child. So, instead of waiting for my kids to ask me to play a game, I became more proactive about suggesting it. I saw the same results at home. Truly, being a TeamMates mentor has been a blessing in every area of my life."

A third mentor said this in regard to his mentoring being of benefit to him as a parent. "Having two children of my own, of a similar age as my mentee, it has allowed me to see a different perspective of what youth of today experience every day, and it has helped me in not only the relationship with my mentee, but also with relationships with my own children."

Adults often assume the world their children face is much the same as what they experienced growing up. However, technology, substance abuse, peer pressure and altered social norms young people face today often make the world a much different and more challenging place than that which adults experienced when they were young. Mentoring which occurs at the school is often particularly eye-opening for those adults who have not recently been in a school building. School populations are more diverse, there are more cultural differences, and many more children come from very difficult family circumstances. Security in schools is much more stringent and concerns about personal safety are heightened in many of our schools. There was a time when a person could just walk into a school without reporting to someone in a supervisory or security position, but this isn't true anymore. Finally this observation from a mentor, "Getting to know my mentee, who is close in age to my own daughter, has benefited my own relationship with my daughter. My mentee communicates things to me that I do not get from my own child."

This mentor's relationship with her mentee has provided a window into the life not only of the mentee, but also the world in which her daughter lives. A mentoring relationship is not encumbered by the sense of ownership and responsibility which often accompanies parenting. Mentors are not burdened with the tendency to see children as extensions of themselves, rather the mentee is removed enough to be seen more objectively, as a separate human being. Mentors are often less tempted to try to "fix" the young person in the way a parent often is. The mentor is free to accept and enjoy the company of the young person being mentored without judgment. A mentor observed: "knowing that I can be there for my mentee in a way her own parents, teachers, peers can't is a rewarding feeling."

3. Mentors often mention that meeting with their mentee brightens their day. "I feel like I have made a difference in (my mentee's) life by being a constant for her. (My mentee) has brightened my day every time I go visit her," said one mentor. Another mentor commented "Seeing her face light up every week is the highlight of my week. I have this incredibly talented and smart young woman who really looks up to me and gets excited to see me every single week." And another said, "The most rewarding aspect of my relationship is the genuine smile I receive every time I first see him in the hallway on a visit, and the feedback from his teachers and relatives that tell me how much he looks forward to seeing me each week."

We find approximately ninety-five percent of our mentees report they trust their mentors and are happy when they are with them. Seeing the response on the faces of the young people being mentored and realizing that they are appreciated is very rewarding to mentors.

One last observation from a mentor: "She is always appreciative of the little things I do such as providing the materials for
a craft we can both work on. She has made a difference in my
life and made me more aware of the challenges children face.
I think I have gotten more from my mentee than I have given
to her. It is rewarding to know the one hour, once a week,
that I spend with my mentee is a bright spot in her day!" We
hear over and over again the sentiment "I have gotten more
from my mentee than I have given to her (or him)." Most
people become mentors anticipating they will do all of the
giving and contributing and are often surprised that they
receive so much from the experience in return.

**4. Most mentors value the relationship they establish
with their mentee.** "I have thoroughly benefited from the
time away from work and getting to know one student on a
deeper level. I feel my time with my mentee is stress free and
allows me to be a kid again! I have enjoyed leaving all the
technology behind and having a friendship with a cool young
person! I feel I keep informed of all the new latest and greatest fashions and trends!"

Often the relationship becomes deeper through hardship and
tragedy. A mentor described an incident which illustrates
this. "The most rewarding part of mentoring has been watching my mentee grow into an amazing, confident and courageous young woman. I was astounded with this young
woman's faith and courage after the unexpected passing of
her father. Her strength is beyond comparison. My mentee is
an amazing young woman."

An important part of the relationship for most mentors is the
realization that the young people being mentored trust them
implicitly. This strong sense of trust helps bind the relationship. It often takes time for trust to be established, but once

it is, it makes the relationship stronger and more meaningful. One mentor expressed this well as follows: "I have had three different TeamMates throughout my years as a mentor and they have all been quite different, but I think the most rewarding or beneficial part of those mentoring relationships is establishing a trusting relationship. Although you may not always like what you hear, it's rewarding to know I can be a support to someone who may really need it and that we can trust and value each other."

Often mentors are appreciative of their relationship with their mentees in that they see them seeking a mentor in an attempt to find meaning and purpose in their existence. One mentor wrote, "What has been most rewarding being a mentor with TeamMates is the ability to build relationships with young men who are trying to find their purpose. It has been such a blessing to be an encouragement to my mentees as they are trying to maneuver through high school and life . . . they are looking to be taken seriously and to be held accountable for their actions. Ultimately, as they are trying to find themselves, they need as many people as possible to help them from the traps of discouragement, temptations, and hopelessness."

5. Mentors often report that mentoring has been educational and informative. They become more aware of some of the issues young people are dealing with which they had not been aware of. Sometimes those issues are difficult to hear about, but the mentor's understanding of the world we live in is expanded. A mentor related, "The most difficult aspect of mentoring is hearing the struggles my mentee goes through at home. I try to have her see the future and how she can change to make a difference.

Another mentor said, "It took me some time to get comfortable listening to their struggles and not feel guilty about the home life my family had. I admit that at first I struggled with the way the boys I mentored would say they didn't see themselves going to school after high school, or weren't even sure why they had to go to school. One of my children is a teacher; one is in medical school. The youngest two are in high school, and we are visiting college campuses. That is more the norm I am used to. To think that a thirteen year old does not see a future for himself, or more importantly, doesn't even have a dream of what they want to be after high school is something I work on every time we are together."

A seventeen year mentor shared four tips for success during his mentoring experience:

Patience: One of the key benefits learned is patience. Often, short term progress by the mentee is hard to see and measure, but with patience and over a period of time positive progress can be measured.

Listening: Another important aspect of mentoring is being a "good listener" and letting the mentee do the talking. This way one can ask questions from points brought up by the mentee to get a better understanding of the mentee's family, needs, home life and goals.

Avoiding Judgment: By not being judgmental about what a mentee tells you about family, home life, needs and goals, over time you use this information as a building block to help move the mentee forward in a positive direction to meet future goals.

Appreciating School Staff: It is easy to criticize what's going on in a school if you've never been inside the doors and seen the effort that occurs on a daily basis to help students. Being a mentor gives one the opportunity to see what the school staff does daily to help students. Developing a working relationship with the staff, and particularly with the mentee's counselor, provides an opportunity to reinforce what the counselor and teachers are doing to help the mentee and be part of a team.

Mentors often are disturbed by the difficulties many of their mentees have, yet at the same time they are becoming more aware of circumstances faced by young people on a daily basis which they had not been exposed to previously. They enter into the lives of their mentees vicariously and experience the pain and also the joys the mentees are experiencing. This awareness makes the mentor more fully human and more understanding of today's culture.

Sometimes a mentor doesn't realize small victories are really major victories in the lives of some children. The story one mentor told illustrates this quite well. "With my first mentee our relationship was great, but he ended up going to alternative school due to continued behavior issues. During that time, we continued our mentoring relationship, and after six months, he was back in school. I felt like I was a total failure when he had to go to alternative school, but as I talked through the issue with our local TeamMates rep, I gradually let go of the failure thoughts. My lesson learned was realizing that each mentee can't become President of the United States. I went into mentoring thinking I could move mountains, when in reality the mentee just wants a positive adult role model in their life. Realizing that just graduating high school is a great achievement took a while to warm up to. Ultimately my mentee did stay in school and graduate, and he now has a great job."

The Journal of Vocational Behavior cited research which found that employees who mentored, compared to colleagues who did not mentor, reported a greater sense of having career success, better job performance, a greater connectedness to their organization and a greater likelihood that they would stay with their employer.

Dr. Susan Weinberger, a noted authority on mentoring, found those who mentor are generally happier, feel better about themselves and often have a fresh perspective on life. She also noted that mentors often feel they benefit from the additional friendship they experience, increase their level of patience with others and learn better relational skills, which are helpful in dealing with their own families.

Nearly every successful person can point to at least one person who has come alongside as a mentor at a critical time and made a major difference in their lives. Young people from all walks of life and all kinds of families can benefit from having a mentor.

Here are a few of the benefits mentors have received from being a mentor:

- pride in seeing the young person grow
- learning how to relate better to young people, including their own children
- experiencing the love and appreciation of the mentee
- creating a long-lasting relationship
- learning more about the world young people live in
- a greater sense of meaning and purpose in their own life.

Serving another in a significant way by giving the most precious gift of all, your time, is one of the most meaningful things a person can do.

CHAPTER SEVEN

COACHING AND MENTORING

Coaching provides a very powerful mentoring opportunity. For an athlete, the season is a microcosm of a lifetime. There is a beginning, with hopes, dreams and aspirations for all that the season holds. Then comes the early training camp with its physical exertion, hard knocks and the first reality check of how one measures up against the competition. Next the season starts, with the even greater challenge of performing against an opponent in game conditions. If your team wins and you are able to contribute to the effort, positive emotions generally result. Confidence in one's own abilities and those of the team start to build. If a player is relegated to a back-up role life gets a little harder, particularly if there appears to be little chance of playing. Even then, being part of a team, something larger than oneself, can be rewarding. If the culture is sound, there is unity of purpose among players and coaches and one can see his or her efforts contributing in some way to the greater good, even a back up role can be significant.

However, things don't always go well. In a negative environment where there is disunity, little opportunity to play and the team is obviously headed nowhere, life gets hard. Sometimes just getting through another practice is difficult.

And then there is the conclusion of the season, or the end of a career. The ending is always abrupt and difficult to adjust to. The player loses his identity as a team member and loses many of the daily associations which have become an important part of a familiar process. He relinquishes the normal routine to which he has grown accustomed, the close friendships, and the flow of adrenaline which competition stirs.

Many players harken back to those days as a team member as some of their finest, maybe even the high point of their existence. Many maintain associations with those who were on the team throughout their lifetime. Those bonds tend to be much stronger than with those one associated with in a chemistry class, a social club, or a dormitory or fraternity.

The reason those athletic-related bonds tend to be very strong is the intensity of shared experiences. Sitting in class or sharing living quarters does not normally involve the intense highs and lows of athletic competition. The physical effort and hardship, the scrutiny of fans and coaches and the testing of one's talents and mettle in a very public arena is very demanding. So, often the end of a season or the end of a playing career can entail a note of relief, but also there is a feeling of loss–loss of identity, loss of camaraderie, loss of pursuing a common goal.

Many cultures have formal rites of passage for their young men and young women, times when they formally move from childhood to early adulthood. In our culture those rites of passage are not as formalized or common, and team membership and athletic accomplishment often takes that place. Unfortunately, not everyone will join a team or be an accomplished athlete. I believe the loss of formal rites of passage has not served our young people well. Many are still living with their parents into their twenties and thirties. The transition from childhood to adulthood is not clearly marked out.

On a positive note, however, it is estimated that nearly fifty million adolescents out of roughly eighty million young people in our nation will have played an organized sport under the supervision of a coach. So, the reach of athletics and role of the coach is very important in the lives of a majority of our young people.

Because of the importance our culture puts on athletic competition and the strong emotions which accompany sports, the coach is in a unique position of influence. The coach determines who makes the team, who plays and who doesn't, the practice routine, the strategies of the game, the team environment and culture and many other things which affect the player's experience.

Therefore, what a coach says and does has a great deal of importance to the young people on the team. For some athletes their coach is the most significant person in their lives.

Grant Teaff, Executive Director of the American Football Coaches Association recently wrote:

". . . . there is an opportunity to teach life's lessons by the very nature of the game. There is no entitlement on a football field. Everything has to be earned. A coach's greatest influence is not so much in what he teaches, but in how his players recognize what he teaches in the way his lives his life.

Coaches have a greater opportunity than ever before to be positive influences in today's society. Coaches are able to use practices and games to teach values and develop positive character qualities in their players. The lessons taught will be validated by the values and character of the teacher."

Because of the coach's position of influence there is the opportunity to do great good in the lives of young people. Unfortunately, there is also the opportunity to do a great deal of harm as well. Most coaches tend to coach in the way they were coached as young athletes. For many coaches the type of coaching they experienced as players was patterned after an authoritarian, boot camp style of coaching which often had its roots in military training. Many coaches came out of a World War II, Korean or Vietnam war experience and their training was often passed on from one generation of coaches to the next. Anyone who has been through basic training or boot camp can harken back to those very difficult months when heads were shaved, beards and mustaches came off, any vestige of individuality or ego was subjected to ridicule and one was treated as an unworthy object to be ordered around and humiliated at every turn.

The philosophy behind this type of training seemed to be predicated on the belief that if a recruit was subjected to harsh training, broken down with all individuality stripped away, then the soldier would be more compliant and accept orders without question, even when great danger and the prospect of death was imminent. This approach was often transferred from a military context to the athletic arena. Athletes were to be good "soldiers" who would conform to team standards, lose individual identity, bear hardship without complaint and be molded into a team which would perform much as a fighting force would. There is some merit to this approach. Who would question adherence to team standards, rigorous training and a subjugation of individuality to the welfare of the team?

Unfortunately, however, this approach also left in its wake a good deal of human carnage. Joe Ehrmann outlines his experience with one of his coaches in his book *Inside Out Coaching*. One of Joe's coaches was very authoritarian.

"Like many ex-military coaches of his generation, he regularly made connections between sports, war, patriotism and manhood. Real men went to war; real men stoically sacrificed their bodies for the good of the team. The team was always first; the opponent was the enemy, and his players were "soldiers" and "warriors" who would "take no prisoners" and "never surrender." Like all good soldiers, we obediently followed orders, never questioning the chain of command. . . . He knew what he wanted out of me, and he knew how to get it. He loved my anger, leveraged my needs, and used my 'mean streak' to serve his mission perfectly."

Joe became an All-American football player and had a distinguished career in the National Football League, but he realizes this particular approach to coaching did not make him a better, more integrated person. Rather it contributed to stoking the anger and hostility within him, which made his life much more difficult and chaotic. Joe's coach had come directly from the military. Many other coaches, although not military men, have been heavily influenced by coaches who were coached by a military boot camp method and the coaching style has rippled down through several generations of coaches. I have heard coaches refer to opponents as "the enemy" and have heard them talking about "taking no prisoners" even though these coaches were never near a military installation.

Fortunately, Joe also had an encounter with a coach who impacted him in a much different way. During his senior year at Syracuse he decided to play lacrosse, and the lacrosse coach made a profound impression on him;

"He was the first person I ever heard make the connection between sports and spirituality. Native Americans call lacrosse "The Creator's Game." My memories of that season were more atmospheric than incidental. There was no shouting, screaming, shaming, or use of sarcasm to control players. Instead there were these sensations: finesse instead of force, camaraderie instead of combat, and an abiding memory that playing and feeling alive were still connected. He took my personal vision from the playing field and turned it up to the sky."

Lacrosse, like football, is a rough game. There is little padding, and physical play is part of the game. Joe was seeing a different way to approach athletic competition, a way that was not dehumanizing but rather uplifting and spiritual in nature.

Many high profile coaches have employed a "take no prisoners" approach, and their success has caused many young coaches to emulate their style. In his book *The Junction Boys,* Jim

Dent chronicles a famous Texas A&M pre-season training camp conducted by coach Paul "Bear" Bryant in the small West-Texas town of Junction in the summer of 1954. Coach Bryant had recently been hired as the head football coach at A&M and decided his team needed to be toughened and disciplined. The upshot was the ten day camp, held in 100 degree plus heat on a barren, rocky, dusty practice field in Junction, roughly three hundred miles west of the A&M campus.

The camp was one of the most grueling, punishing and brutal camps ever held. One hundred and fifteen players rode buses to Junction and only thirty five came back as members of the team. The rest had quit, many leaving in the middle of the night, hitch-hiking home. Water breaks were not allowed, and the players were driven to the point of complete exhaustion and dehydration. Injuries were largely ignored. Even though none of the players died, they were pushed to the brink.

The legend surrounding the Junction experience has grown with time. It is embedded in Texas football culture as an example of what it takes to mold a great team. What is often lost in the narrative is the fact that the 1954 Texas A&M team won only one game. That A&M won a conference championship two years later is cited as validation for what occurred at Junction.

In fairness to Coach Bryant, he expressed some regret in his later years about the way players were treated at Junction and indicated he owed them an apology. However, the legend of Junction looms large in the minds of many coaches. Anxious to emulate the success Bear Bryant enjoyed as a coach, some have adopted an approach to coaching which, although not as extreme as the Junction experience, echoes a similar philosophy.

Many claim that separating out the "quitters" and molding the "winners" into a close unit at Junction provided the foundation for later success. There may have been some value in the experience for some of the players who survived the camp.

However, there were eighty who would always bear the label of "quitter," those who didn't measure up when things got tough. I would imagine as the stories about Junction proliferated and were embellished, those eighty players at times felt like failures and carried those scars to their graves. Surely there were some courageous and skilled players among those eighty, who, under the right circumstances, would have made a contribution to their team.

Every person has a breaking point, a point where they can no longer go on. One person may break down due to physical pain, another is more vulnerable to psychological suffering caused by humiliation or a vague perceived threat and yet another may dissolve when isolated and alone. No one falls neatly into compartments labeled "quitters" and "winners." In the right set of circumstances, the "quitter" can be brave and accomplish great things. In some circumstances the "winner" will buckle and fail miserably. Much depends on how people are treated and how they view their situation.

Coaching plays a major role in determining whether a player grows and develops as a result of athletic competition or is somehow diminished and frustrated. A coach who sees himself as a mentor, an educator, one who is trying to accomplish greater maturity and balance in the lives of his players, can be a very positive presence in the lives of those he coaches.

A coach who is obsessed with the bottom line and sees his main purpose in coaching as winning games at any cost can do great damage. The paradox lies with the fact that if a coach doesn't win often enough, he won't last long in the coaching profession. There is a tension between doing what is best for one's athletes and what is perceived to be best regarding the win-loss record. Even though a coach may want to treat his players with respect and mentor them in a way that develops their character and personal growth, he may be afraid to alter his approach because he has experienced only an authoritarian, top-down, "our opponent is the enemy" coaching style. Therefore he is afraid to depart from it for fear that he will not be able to win enough games. So the coach is stuck with the survival instinct and fails to venture out into the uncharted territory of coaching as a mentor and a teacher.

There is the fear of being "soft." Baseball manager Leo Durocher said many years ago, "nice guys finish last," and many coaches, whether they have heard that actual quote or not, subscribe to the belief that without a tough-guy approach they won't be successful.

So what does it mean to mentor as a coach? First it doesn't mean you are not well versed in tactics, fundamentals and game strategy. It doesn't mean you are not committed to a disciplined environment in which players are on time, adhere to team standards, and practice hard. It doesn't mean players are coddled and shielded from the harsh realities of competition.

What it does mean is that you care about your players beyond the won-loss record. You are concerned about their well-being, their health, their education, their developing into young people with character, their willingness to serve a cause larger than themselves.

The coach, by design or not, will create a culture within the team. The culture may be uplifting, devoid of personal attacks and humiliation, in which players are treated with respect and encouraged to improve and achieve great things. Or, in contrast, the culture may be one of dog-eat-dog competition in which there is little positive reinforcement but rather a relentless obsession with winning in which players are treated as though they are pawns on a chessboard being manipulated to gain recognition for the coach.

Tony Dungy, former coach of the Tampa Bay Buccaneers and the Indianapolis Colts, wrote *The Mentor Leader* in which he outlines the importance of mentoring in the coaching profession. "We often mirror what we see. Coaches will model the behavior of successful coaches they know or observe, sometimes with detrimental results. . . . Too often, though, we choose people to mirror or model, and leadership books to read, solely for the purpose of figuring out how to win games or increase our financial bottom line. In the process of looking for leadership models to emulate, we choose people who have won a lot of games or who have made a lot of money for themselves or their organizations, with little thought given to how they have affected the lives of people around them. If along the way lives are made better, we too often view it as a wonderful byproduct rather than a primary purpose of leadership."

Tony believes the primary focus of the coach should be that of mentoring and bettering the lives of his players. If done well, this approach will often lead to success on the scoreboard as well, but winning should not be the primary focus. I'm certain many fans would be horrified to hear of this approach to coaching; however, I agree with Tony. Helping players mature and become better human beings is not antithetical to having success on the field of play; oftentimes they go hand in hand.

I have always admired John Wooden, the extraordinarily gifted former coach of the UCLA basketball team. Through one of the most remarkable stretches of basketball history ever recorded by a college team, John's teams won the NCAA basketball tournament an amazing ten out of twelve years. During that time his UCLA team won eighty eight games in a row, home and away, a record which will likely never be broken.

I believe John was able to accomplish this extraordinary record primarily because he was so well grounded philosophically. Most coaches can tell you what they do in the way of drills, offensive and defensive schemes and tactics, but few can clearly state *why* they do what they do. It is difficult for a coach to lead effectively if he has not come to terms with himself, is not comfortable with who he is and is not certain of his own value system and coaching philosophy. A coach who is insecure and is constantly vacillating with the demands of parents, fans and the media will have a very difficult time staying the course and leading his team in a consistent, positive manner.

John Wooden, like Tony Dungy, saw coaching as mentoring. In his book *A Game Plan for Life: The Power of Mentoring,* John is quoted as saying, "he made his living as a coach but lived his life to be a mentor." He felt that a mentor (coach) was one who models life principles. A mentor teaches about humility, contentment, interactions with family and friends, and keeping priorities straight in a world that often threatens to invert them.

John was fond of pointing out that his father gave him a creed when he graduated from the eighth grade which provided him a compass by which to live his life and guided him through the challenges of coaching. The creed is as follows:

Be true to yourself
Help others
Make friendship a fine art
Drink deeply from good books, especially the Bible
Make each day your masterpiece
Build a shelter against a rainy day by the life that you live
Give thanks for your blessings and pray for guidance every day

Fortunately, John didn't lose the handwritten note his father gave him containing the seven principles but rather incorporated them into his daily life and based his life on the wisdom they contained.

Somewhere I have a signed copy of John's Pyramid For Success, a pyramid of fourteen principles which build upon each other until one arrives at the apex of the pyramid and the final principle, Competitive Greatness. Through a lifetime of coaching John developed, revised and perfected the pyramid, which stated clearly his philosophy of striving for excellence as a coach.

As a result of much reflection and experience he came to know what he believed was important as a coach, both in coaching basketball and in helping his players grow and mature as young men. I was only in his presence a handful of times, but I was greatly influenced by the principles with which he coached and conducted his personal life.

One of those principles, which made a huge difference in the way I coached, was this: John never mentioned winning to his teams. This seemed paradoxical in that John was possibly the most successful coach of all time in terms of winning basketball games, yet he never mentioned the importance of winning to his players. Instead he talked about the "process," the journey that leads to competitive excellence.

He started his first practice session of each season by demonstrating to his players how they should put on their socks so they would avoid blisters. Then he progressed to demonstrating how to pass, how to shoot, dribble, play defense. His premise was that if players mastered fundamentals and had the right practice habits, winning would take care of itself.

I understood what he was saying. If I told our team they "had to win this game," they would understand I thought the game was very important but wouldn't have any greater understanding of what they were to do in order to win the game. As a result, we broke the game down into a series of twelve measurable offensive goals, eleven measurable defensive goals and seven kicking goals. Each of those goals related to things we did in practice each day of the week.

We practiced with those goals in mind. For example, one of those goals was to have no offensive turnovers in a game. Therefore, we practiced carrying the ball "high and tight" in practice.

Ball carriers were to carry the ball high and locked against their chest. We emphasized recovering fumbles any time the ball was on the ground. We practiced having our defensive players "strip" the ball from offensive ball carriers. We wouldn't allow the quarterback to pass the ball into tight spaces where interceptions were likely. In short, we practiced taking care of the ball every day. This led to our being a low turnover team and certainly helped us win, as turnovers are a key football statistic in determining which team wins and which team loses.

We talked about "taking care of the ball" and didn't say "don't fumble" or "don't throw interceptions". It is important to emphasize what you want, not what you don't want.

Our team reviewed the number of goals we accomplished when we met after each game the following Monday. If we met eighty or ninety percent of our goals, we had played well. If we met only fifty percent of our goals or less, we didn't play well. We might have won the game by a large margin, but if we didn't hit most of those target goals we would know that we had under-achieved, and this would eventually catch up to us as the season progressed. The object was to play well, to perform at a high level—the goals were a way we could measure what a high level of performance looked like in quantifiable terms.

John Wooden defined success much differently than most do. "Success is peace of mind, which is a direct result of self-satisfaction in knowing you made the effort to become the best of which you are capable. Success is never final; failure is never fatal. It's courage that counts."

Coaching is very difficult in that a coach is nearly always measured exclusively by the number of wins and losses he or she accumulates during a career. The win-loss record is nearly always mentioned prominently in one's obituary or upon the occasion of being fired or hired in a new position.

Over time, I began to adhere more closely to John's definition of success than the way most people measure athletic accomplishment. It was always painful to lose a game, but if I knew we had done everything in our power to prepare well, the team attitude and chemistry was right, and we had given a maximum effort, then, in a very real sense we had won, regardless of what the scoreboard might say. On the other hand, we might have had more points than our opponent, but if we had not played up to our capability, we had failed.

We lost two national championship games in which we played very well, played well enough to win. Where many were devastated by those losses, and I must admit I was hurting too, I took a good deal of satisfaction in knowing we had played at the highest level of college football and played well enough to win. Grantland Rice, a prominent sportswriter more than seventy years ago, wrote, "For when the One Great Scorer comes to write against your name, it matters not that you won or lost, but how you played the game."

I'm afraid Grantland Rice's take on what is most important in athletics may seem too idealistic and out of touch with reality to many contemporary observers of the athletic landscape. However, I believe what he said is absolutely true and is as relevant today as it was seventy plus years ago when the words were first written. Sometimes a team loses because of an incorrect officiating call, an injury or illness, a strange bounce of the ball. These are factors beyond the team's control. If you have prepared properly, have the right attitude and have given maximum effort on the things within your control, then you are successful in the truest sense of the word.

Many times coaches drive themselves out of coaching due to obsessing over wins and losses. A coach will never win enough to satisfy everyone. The more he wins, the higher the expectations. Eventually there is no upside left, only downside. If the coach is able to re-define success in terms of process, however, how well his team performed given its capabilities, coaching does not entail as much heartache and burnout.

My wife Nancy and I visited John Wooden in his apartment in Encino, California, just five months before he died at the age of ninety nine. He was still very sharp, very kind and, as always, a true gentleman. He wanted us to have lunch with him at his favorite restaurant near by, where he often met his former players when they came to visit him. It seems his former players came to appreciate him and valued his influence on them even more as the years went by.

Pat Williams quotes Andy Hill, one of John Wooden's former players, in his book, *Coach Wooden*. In reflecting on the impact John had on his players Andy Hill said, "coach never talked about that seven-point creed around us. He didn't need to. He lived that creed. He was that creed. And because he was, his players got those principles from him without even realizing it. When you truly live your creed you don't have to talk about it."

Pat Williams also quotes Jamaal Wilkes, one of UCLA's greatest players, "Help others–that principle really sums up John Wooden's life. His example has impacted me greatly. When you help others, you don't do it expecting anything in return. You just help people because it's the right thing to do. Yet it always seems to work out that when you help other people, you help yourself as well."

Speaking at John Wooden's memorial service Kareem Abdul-Jabbar is quoted as saying: "There were so many things I learned from Coach over my lifetime, but the things that mattered most were family and faith. . . . He never swore at us and never talked to us about winning. Even while winning all those championships, Coach was more concerned about having a positive effect on the lives of all the young men who played for him. Coach's value system was from another era."

A coach's influence often isn't fully understood or appreciated until an athlete has graduated and gone on with his life. I often heard former players comment on the fact that they didn't fully realize the importance of what they learned and experienced during their playing careers until they had moved on, were involved in their careers and were raising families themselves. Lee Kunz, a linebacker who played on some of the first teams I coached, said this when interviewed for the book *Heart of a Husker:* "I was influenced by Tom a lot more than I initially realized when I was there. That was a big part of our lives, and he was a father figure to a lot of the team." I never thought of myself as a father figure or a role model, but with the passage of time and with the benefit of talking to many former players years after they played I realize that a coach, by the nature of his position, is uniquely placed in a position of influence.

A coach can influence by the words he speaks, but his greatest impact lies in his actions, the way he conducts his life more than with the words he speaks. Young people are quick to detect inconsistencies between what a coach says and what he does. Players are able to observe their coaches in the best of times and the worst of times. They watch closely how the coach reacts when they have just won a big game or have lost the championship, when fans are pleased with the team and also when the public is calling for the coach's head. They see the coach when all the players are healthy and playing well and when injuries have taken a toll and performance has fallen off. They watch how he reacts in the heat of a tight game, and they observe his reaction when an official makes a questionable call or when a player makes a costly error.

So what are some of the ways a coach can make a difference?

1. Integrity

There are two components of integrity, honesty and keeping promises. When I became a head coach in 1973 there was a substantial amount of dishonesty in recruiting athletes. Some schools were offering cash, clothes and automobiles. Many schools would not break NCAA rules but enough did to make it a very uneven playing field. There was always the temptation to join the cheating as some of those schools were highly successful and difficult to beat. Early on, however, we determined that we would not break the rules even if it meant we would lose our jobs.

If one of the earliest experiences a player had with a coaching staff involved an illegal inducement the message being sent was that dishonesty was acceptable and part of the culture of a team. This is a very bad way to start a coach-player relationship as it tells the player the way to achieve success is to break the rules.

In addition to offers of illegal inducements involving money or extra benefits, promises of playing time were often made to recruits. Some were promised a starting position as a freshman, being on the travel squad the first year, even that the coach would change his offense or defense to accommodate the skills of an unproven recruit. Such promises were not NCAA violations, but they were unethical because they were not based on performance on the field and, if kept, were unfair to other players who were competing for playing time.

We didn't promise players anything but an opportunity to play if they proved themselves. We lost some players because we didn't tell them what they wanted to hear, but many of those players were the right ones to lose because they were players who were looking for a deal, a short cut. For the most part the right ones came, those who were willing to work their way onto the field. They often said they appreciated that they weren't offered anything illegal or promised immediate playing time when they were recruited at Nebraska. They knew some of the promises they were hearing from other schools did not ring true.

We also believed it was extremely important to be honest with our players once they had enrolled and were on the team. We explained why they were at a certain spot on the depth chart and what they needed to do to move up. We made sure we followed through when we told a player something. We also insisted on academic integrity.

We told our walk-on players they would receive a scholarship if they were first or second on the depth chart at the end of fall camp. We saved three or four scholarships each year so we could honor those promises. This wasn't easy to do, as there were always more high school recruits who could be added to the roster by using those scholarships we were saving. The walk-on player who had proven himself worthy and had paid a great price to climb the depth chart was a much surer investment of a scholarship than an unproven recruit, however.

Where there is integrity there will be a high degree of trust. It is very difficult to have a great organization without a high level of trust. I am certain those coaches who demonstrated a lack of integrity in dealing with their players did not have great morale among their team. Some of those coaches won championships fairly quickly and were very popular with fans, but I noticed they often didn't have long careers and had a difficult time sustaining their programs and keeping their jobs. Those coaches who lasted, whose careers spanned a substantial number of years, usually did things the right way.

A person in a position of authority can often appear to get away with saying one thing and doing another because they are the coach or they are the boss and people are afraid to challenge their authority. However, bad behavior is always duly noted and confidence in their leadership and integrity is eroded. Eventually they lose their moral authority and the respect of those they lead.

2. Consistency

It is always disconcerting to people when their leader is erratic, up one day and down the next, constantly changing goals and plans, treating people differently depending on how the leader feels.

Our coaching staff wrote a mission statement indicating our goals, our core values and how people were going to be treated. We reviewed the mission statement at the beginning of each football season, sometimes tweaking it, but for the most part it stayed pretty much the same. We looked at the mission statement periodically throughout the year to make sure we were staying true to its principles. The mission statement wasn't written by the head coach; it was a document which was discussed, analyzed and agreed upon by our entire coaching staff.

According to our mission statement, our players were to be given a place of central importance. We wanted to make sure their education came first, their health was not to be compromised, we were not to humiliate or denigrate them, but rather we were to teach them as best we could to be good players and build their confidence whenever possible. We were to treat everyone with respect: players, coaches, support staff, the media, the fans. We were going to be as thorough as possible in preparing for each game. Each opponent was to get our full attention.

We followed nearly the same routine each week, win or lose. We emphasized process over end results. The important thing was how we played: displaying sound technique and fundamentals, team unity, exceptional effort, self-control. We felt if we did those things well the final score would take care of itself. We measured performance by how well we played and how close we came to playing a perfect game, not by the final score. There were times we lost but played about as well as we could play; we recognized this with the players and complimented them on their playing at a high level. There were times we won but did not play well, and we expressed concern about the things we did not do well, as those things would eventually trip us up if we didn't address them.

It was important to maintain a fairly even temperament throughout a game. A coach who is out of control emotionally can't help its team play well. In such cases the team often mirrors their coach's instability and falls apart as well. The only thing that got me riled up was a lack of effort, as that is something a team is always expected to give. A player might fumble, miss a tackle or drop a pass, but nobody felt worse about the mistake than that player, so I didn't come down on them for those kinds of mistakes. Rather, I tried to encourage them. If the mistake was caused by lack of proper technique, we would correct the mistake and express confidence in his ability to get things right the next time.

Games, contrary to popular belief, are not won because of a fiery pre-game or half-time speech or ranting and raving on the sideline. They are won by effective practice on Monday, Tuesday, Wednesday, Thursday and Friday. It also helps if the coaches have their wits about them enough to make proper adjustments during the game itself, and a high level of emotion is often not helpful in making those adjustments. A coach has to keep his head in the game and constantly anticipate the next move the opponent will make. I believe our players realized the importance of a steady, persistent, thorough approach to the game. Many have said they have used this approach later in their professional lives and with their families.

3. Language

We live in a culture which seems to be more profane than previous generations. We see and hear language used in our media outlets which would not have been allowed over the airwaves or in print twenty or thirty years ago. It seems our young people have been impacted to a great degree by the barrage of explicit language they are continually exposed to. Words which were seldom used at one time because of their offensiveness are now commonplace.

I remember visiting with a lady getting along in years who worked at the ticket office in the athletic department of a large university. She was hearing the same especially offensive word being used over and over again as a part of normal conversation by students who were buying student tickets. She finally exploded on one young man and told him she had been hearing that word for hours; she was tired of it and didn't want to hear it anymore. She said the young man seemed surprised at her outburst and was apologetic; he did not seem to be aware that the language he was using was inappropriate. There was a time when foul language was not to be used in public, particularly in the presence of a lady. That day seems to be over.

Unfortunately, profanity is commonly used by many coaches, and this contributes to the perception by their

Reverend J B Currens, my grandfather's mentor, a strong influence on my grandfather, and, indirectly, me as well.

My grandfather, Tom Osborne, as a young minister.

My mother, father, brother Jack and me just before my dad left for World War II.

Scrap metal my second grade class gathered for the war effort.
I am fifth from the left, front row, with my bib overalls.

Bob Devaney and I were together for thirty years.

Nancy and me with John Wooden shortly before he passed away at age ninety nine.

My mentor and friend Woody Varner (center).

Last game as a coach, 1998 Orange Bowl against Tennessee.

Charlie McBride, Ron Brown, Milt Tenopir (seated) and me along with members of the 1994 team, celebrating their 20 year anniversary of a National Championship.

Brook Berringer, a great player and a great person.

Tommie Frazier, number 15, a great competitor.

Scott Frost quarterbacked us to an undefeated season in 1997.

players that it is acceptable. Some of the great coaches such as John Wooden, football coach Bobby Bowden and others seemed to be able to coach effectively and communicate meaningfully without being profane. When John Wooden was especially excited I understand he would say "goodness gracious, sakes alive" as his strongest verbal admonition. Bobby Bowden's strongest word was "dadgummit." Both coaches were able to get their point across well enough that they won multiple national championships and are listed among the great coaches of all time.

A coach is first and foremost a teacher. It would be unusual to hear a classroom teacher utter a string of profanities, and I would submit that it should be equally unusual on the athletic field. In order to elicit the correct response from his athletes, a coach must be very clear in explaining what he wants the player to do. If the player does not do what is desired the coach can put the player on the bench. He doesn't have to get angry or become profane, he simply rewards those who follow instruction with more playing time and those who don't do what is required with less playing time.

We often hear of coaching being referred to as a "profession." If coaching is truly a profession, then a coach should act like a professional and use the language a professional person would use. Sometimes coaches may feel profanity adds emphasis to what they are saying or makes them appear tougher or more authoritarian. My experience has been that those who feel profanity is necessary to bolster their "tough" image often really aren't that secure in who they are and adopt a false bravado, often laced with profanity, to cover their insecurity.

Of great importance in effective teaching and mentoring is being positive. The best way to change behavior is to catch someone doing something correctly and praise what they are doing. Tearing people down, humiliating and denigrating them, has no place in a good learning environment. When a coach continually engages in criticism, particularly when that criticism gets personal, players often tune the coach out. The player uses the tuning out process as a defense mechanism to preserve some semblance of dignity and self-worth. No one can endure constant personal attacks without using a defensive strategy.

4. Values

As my time in coaching progressed I became more and more aware of the fact that many of the concepts I was trying to communicate to my players did not resonate with them. To many of them the term "honesty" had more to do with not getting caught than with telling the truth and keeping one's word. They understood what "courage" meant when it came to physical bravery but had little understanding of what moral courage was–the courage to endure ridicule or ostracism for doing the right thing. Similarly, the meaning of words such as loyalty, generosity, self-sacrifice and accountability were not very clear to many of them.

I had gotten to know Marty Shottenheimer, coach of the Kansas City Chiefs professional football team, and he told me he had been presenting his players with a "theme of the week," a concept he wanted to emphasize during the week's preparation for an upcoming opponent. I thought this approach would work well in presenting different character traits to my players I wanted them to understand more clearly.

So each week we introduced a character trait on Monday during our team meeting. We would have it written prominently in the weekly scouting report on our upcoming opponent. We would have two or three quotes from well-known people referring to the character trait, and then I would make some mention of the trait each day during our team meeting which would further explain what the trait might mean to each player and to our team.

For example, the theme for a week might be "courage." We included a quote attributed to former Green Bay Packer Coach Vince Lombardi, "fatigue makes cowards of us all." His quote referred to the fact that when a player was exhausted he could no longer do the brave thing, pursue the football on defense or block downfield on offense. We also included a quote from Confucius which said "to see what is right and not do it is a lack of courage." This quote obviously referred to moral courage, a willingness to do the right thing even though it might be unpopular. We then gave examples of what physical courage and moral courage might look like in their daily lives and what those concepts might mean to our team.

In the course of a thirteen or fourteen week season our players were presented with a thorough explanation of thirteen or fourteen different character traits and what those traits might mean to them personally and to our team. In short, they took a character education course, even though we didn't label it as such.

I think it made a difference. Occasionally I would see a player quoted in the newspaper or overhear a conversation between players in which they would relate something which had been presented in reference to a character trait. I think it helped our team chemistry, as it caused players to be more conscious of values which bind people together and made them more willing to sacrifice personal objectives in order to serve others.

The family unit has been compromised by a lack of parenting. For some players the coach is the only one who can impart sound teaching on matters related to character. Many times the coach is the one authority figure who commands respect and is also involved in something so important to athletes, their sport, that they will pay close attention.

5. Dealing with adversity

One thing is certain about athletics; there will be adversity. One thing is also certain about life in general; there will be adversity. Adversity presents a coach with a great opportunity to mentor and teach his players. Players will be injured, games will be lost, there may be a death in the family, a girlfriend may decide to break up. We tried to minimize the damage adversity causes and capitalize instead on the opportunities adversity presents.

It may be an oversimplification, but I noticed people usually handle adversity in one of three ways. They quit, they blame others or circumstances, or they see opportunity. When a person is demoted from the first team to the third team, that person may quit the team by leaving the team or he may quit by no longer trying to improve and putting forth effort. Another player who is demoted may blame the coach who demoted him, claiming the coach plays favorites, is stupid, bears a grudge against the player, or is simply incompetent. Still another player encountering the same fate may see his demotion as an opportunity to learn from the experience, to correct some things he was doing wrong, to improve his commitment and effort.

It is obvious that quitting is not going to accomplish anything if the goal is to be a good player who gets more playing time. Blaming someone else is equally counterproductive. It may make the person feel better to cast the blame on someone else, but it doesn't improve the situation. The only response that results in a positive outcome is seeing adversity as an opportunity to improve and get better, to learn something from the experience.

Most people can relate experiences where a team, a business, or even a family that had an opportunity to grow and benefit from what was learned as a result of a setback, instead unraveled and fell apart because people either quit or were consumed by finger pointing and blaming.

When discussing the way one might deal with adversity, I often reflect on something that happened to our 1996 football team. We were coming off two consecutive unbeaten, national championship seasons in which we had won twenty six straight games. We played Arizona State in Tempe, a team we had beaten badly the year before in Lincoln. It was a very bad night for the University of Nebraska football team; we were humiliated 19-0. We played poorly on offense, making all kinds of mistakes and committing several turnovers. Our defense wasn't that bad, but it was not real sharp either.

Given the fact that we had two straight undefeated seasons, had worked very hard and were shooting for an unprecedented third consecutive national championship, it would have been easy for the team to quit, to reflect on how hard they worked during the preceding seasons and now, with a loss and little prospect of another national championship, to simply shut things down, go through the motions and enjoy themselves the rest of the season. It also would have been very easy to blame others.

However, we assembled the players at our normal meeting time the following Monday and informed them that even though we had not played well, the loss was going to be a very good thing. This would serve as a great learning experience since our weaknesses had been exposed. We had become complacent. We had assumed some areas of our team were good which weren't. We were going to take this experience and become a great team as we worked to improve the deficiencies that had been exposed in the game. Rather than giving up or pointing the finger at others, the players began to look at that game as an opportunity to grow and get better.

We did improve a great deal. We ran off nine straight wins and nearly got into the national championship game for the fourth consecutive year. This example involves losing a football game, hardly a major tragedy, although it felt like it at the time. There are many examples of a much more serious nature.

I recall meeting a mother and father who experienced the devastating loss of a daughter to acute alcohol poisoning while she was in college. They resolved to make something positive of their tragedy and devoted much of their lives to speaking to young people about the dangers of alcohol abuse. Their story was particularly impactful because it was something they had experienced personally, and one could sense the immense pain they felt due to the loss of a daughter. One could readily detect how difficult it was for them to relate the details which led up to their daughter's death, but it was also obvious they found that by being vulnerable and reliving the tragedy they were able to impact others and possibly avert similar tragedies in the lives of other young people.

I think many of our players learned adversity and tragedy can be very instructional and can usually be turned into something positive if they responded in the right way–by trying to learn from the adversity instead of quitting or blaming someone else.

6. Work Ethic

Not being located in a heavily populated state (Nebraska has approximately 1.8 million people) it was difficult to find large numbers of highly skilled quality athletes close by. Therefore it became very important for us to develop the talent we had. We were generally acknowledged to be the first university to have a full-time strength coach, and we were also recognized as having the best strength and conditioning program in the country for many years. Since our strength and conditioning program was so widely recognized our strength coach, Boyd Epley, sent more than sixty assistants to other major universities and professional teams as head strength and conditioning coaches.

Boyd was a great motivator. He had records for all major weightlifting lifts, vertical jump data, agility drill and forty yard dash times posted in our weight room. It became a very big thing when someone broke a record and had his record and picture posted on the wall. We also were credited with having the first full time nutritionist working with our student athletes, and soon nutrition became a major emphasis for most major athletic departments.

We had one other factor working for us. Since we were the only major college football program in the state, we had large numbers of quality athletes who were willing to forgo scholarships at smaller colleges in order to "walk-on." Many of those players grew up wanting to play at Nebraska, and they were willing to pay a great price to realize their dream. Many of them came from farms and small towns and had worked hard all of their lives. The work ethic of these players became contagious. When some highly recruited players from other states saw how hard the walk-ons worked, they began to realize that if they didn't work equally hard they could be passed up by players who may not have had as much innate ability but who would pay a greater price and out-work them. The walk-ons gave us depth, and many of them also became great players, but the greatest contribution they made was to the culture of the team; it was truly a blue collar team committed to outworking opponents.

We recruited walk-on players just as hard as we did scholarship players; we visited their high schools, were in their homes and invited them to our home games. As previously mentioned, we saved three to four scholarships each year for walk-ons who proved their ability to contribute significantly. Walk-ons at Nebraska, unlike many other programs, were treated the same as scholarship players. Most players did not know which of their peers were scholarship players and which were walk-ons. Where you were from, what your high school reputation was, whether you were receiving financial aid or not made no difference. What mattered was your performance, and the harder one worked the better the performance.

A strong work ethic was important for the players, but it was equally important for the coaching staff. Due to the lack of population in Nebraska, recruiting was a year-round, non-stop activity. We had to travel the entire nation in our recruiting efforts, establishing good rapport with high school coaches in many states evaluating thousands of players on high school films, and visiting hundreds of high schools and living rooms across the nation.

We also had to be very thorough in our preparation for our opponents during the season. Our objective was to be exhaustive in preparing for every possible scenario that could conceivably play out on the upcoming Saturday. Details such as how we could best block a punt, get to the quarterback with a given blitz and block a certain stunt we were apt to see, were examined in detail. We came in early, worked late and normally spent eighty to ninety hours each week preparing for a game. There is no excuse for lack of preparation, and hopefully, our players saw that we were putting in the same effort they were.

Most players left our program with an appreciation for the price everyone paid to have a successful program. Many have commented to me since leaving that this has carried over to their business careers and their lives after football.

7. Spirituality

Spirituality has to do with finding a purpose and meaning greater than one's own self interest. For many this has to do with faith in God, for others it may mean dedication to an organization or cause which they see being larger than themselves. I came to realize that football is played in three dimensions, one of which could be considered spiritual.

First, there is the physical component. Blocking and tackling often results in violent collisions; speed is important, and eye-hand coordination is necessary in throwing and catching a football. Strength is important; most football players work very hard in the weight room. Most people think only of the physical nature of the game when they think of football.

Second, there is the mental part of the game. Offensive systems, defensive schemes, audibles and adjustments during a play are critical. Most playbooks are as thick as a good sized phone book. Football is a much more cerebral game than most people realize. If a player does not know what his assignment is on a given play, things fall apart very quickly.

Third, football is not just played with the body and the mind; the heart and soul are also an important part of effective competition. A player who is totally self-absorbed is often a detriment to a team's performance as a unit. A basketball player who shoots the ball every time he touches it, or a football player who is more interested in making a big play and attracting attention rather than doing his job on a specific play is usually a liability. A player who is totally committed to the game, who plays with the proper spirit, will not hold back and will play at a higher level.

Some players seek to honor God with the way they play. They are unselfish, they treat opponents with respect, they don't trash talk, and they give maximum effort. They try to play the way they believe God would have them play. Many fans might say that nobody actually plays the game of football this way. However, I have known many who did, and they were among the best players we had. They were great contributors.

One such player was Brook Berringer, a young man from Goodland, Kansas. Brook stepped in for our first team quarterback, Tommie Frazier, when Tommie was injured during the early part of the 1994 season and was out for nearly all the rest of the season. Brook exceeded all expectations. He led us to seven straight wins, playing at a very high level, and persevering through two instances in which he suffered collapsed lung injuries.

At the end of the season, undefeated, we played Miami for the national championship. Tommie Frazier had recovered enough to play and he and Brook both contributed to the win, which capped a perfect season and the National Championship.

The next year both Tommie and Brook were seniors

and both had earned the right to be starters. Tommie won the starting job by outperforming Brook by a very slim margin in the fall camp prior to the 1995 season. Tommie then led us to another perfect season and another national championship. Brook played sparingly and didn't start a game, but he didn't complain, didn't cause disruption, did the right things, said the right things and was a very valuable part of the team. Brook was a committed Christian and even though not starting hurt him deeply, he wasn't going to act in ways which were contrary to his faith. He was going to contribute to the welfare of the team in any way he could, even if that meant supporting Tommie and the other players from the sideline.

Three months after the season ended Brook was killed while piloting a small plane that crashed in a field near Lincoln. His death had a tremendous impact on our players, primarily because of the way he lived his life, his Christian witness. He was a very good example of how a person's faith, a willingness to honor God in all circumstances, can make a difference. The reason his death was so impactful was not just because he was critical to winning the national championship in 1994, but rather because of the example of selflessness which he displayed during the 1995 season. Team members knew his faith was a key component of who he was and how he lived his life.

We wanted those who were so inclined to have a chance to develop and nurture their faith. We had chapel and mass the morning of each game. We had a silent prayer in the locker room before and after each game, and we had a short devotional period for our coaches and staff each morning before we started preparing for the day. Please don't get the impression that we forced matters of faith on anyone. We simply recognized spiritual support would be important to many of our players and made resources available to them which would nurture their spiritual growth.

A byproduct of spirituality which became apparent was that many players began to put team welfare before personal goals and aspirations. Many of them gave great effort on the scout team for as long as four years, with very little playing time. Some of these players were people of faith and others were not, but they seemed to find added meaning and purpose in their lives by contributing to the welfare of the team, even if, like Brook, they had to sacrifice to make the team stronger.

This willingness to serve others became very powerful. It was woven into our culture and was almost palpable in its effect on the program. Having our players perform community service, both individually and as a team, was part of our Life Skills program. Some spoke to younger children in the schools, some visited the sick and elderly in hospitals and nursing homes, and some served as mentors to children. We felt having our players understand that service to others is a key to a meaningful and successful life was very important to their development as people of character. Sometimes athletics can be "all about me." Moving athletes away from preoccupation with themselves and instilling concern for others was very important to them living lives which were meaningful and not totally self-absorbed.

Some may believe this discussion of spirituality is soft and antithetical to hard-nosed football, which thrives on anger and aggression toward opponents; nice guys really don't win. However, love is the most powerful emotion. It is stronger than hate. A team bound together by mutual love and concern will have greater team unity, a willingness to sacrifice for each other. Great teams are usually set apart by exceptional team chemistry; talent carries a team only so far and there are many talented teams. Great team chemistry based on love and respect comes from the spirit.

8. Leadership

Leadership style is very important in determining the impact the coach will have on his team. The most common leadership style is transactional leadership, which is based primarily on reward and punishment. If a player is attentive, works hard, and does what the coach wants, the player is rewarded with more playing time. If a player fails to perform well, gives little effort, or does not comply with team rules, the player gets less playing time or may even be cut from the team.

Transactional leadership is based upon authoritarian principles. The coach is very much the boss, and what the coach says or wants is to be followed to the letter or there will be negative consequences. This style of leadership is very much top down, and players usually have very little input or control over what will happen on the team. There is usually a heavy emphasis on final results, winning or losing; the final score is the bottom line and is usually all that matters. Former Green Bay Packer coach Vince Lombardi is often quoted as having said "winning isn't everything, it's the only thing." Some have tried to soften Vince's quote by claiming what he really meant was that giving the effort to win was the only thing. However Vince's quote might have been intended, the original version has been quoted so often that many coaches have come to believe winning really is the only thing—nothing else matters.

It is impossible to coach, teach, or run a business without some element of transactional leadership. A coach has to determine who plays and who doesn't, a teacher has a grading system and an employer has to determine who gets paid more than others. However, there is another style of leadership which differs from transactional leadership in significant ways, ways which can lead to optimal growth and performance within a team.

Research has shown that something called transformational leadership is generally most effective in creating an environment in which top performance occurs. Transformational leadership is also often referred to as servant leadership. The leader is not a top-down, authoritarian figure but rather one who serves those who follow. Followers are not pawns on a chessboard whose only purpose is to serve the needs of the leader, rather they are of central importance and the leader seeks to ensure they are cared for, nurtured, and enabled to realize their full potential.

Transformational leadership is principle oriented. Certain core values are emphasized and considered inviolate. Even if a team's chances of winning might be jeopardized if those core values are upheld, even if a business is likely to lose a great deal of money if values are strictly observed, the core principles and values will be maintained. Those values are seen as guidelines which will lead to greater long-term accomplishment if they are observed. Short cuts and bending the rules are not tolerated.

A transformational leader leads by example. If long hours are required, the leader works even longer hours. If integrity is a core value, the leader is ethical in every aspect of his behavior. If things have gone badly for the team or the organization, the leader takes responsibility. If there is personal or financial risk, the leader puts his neck on the line first. The leader does not ask anyone to do anything he himself is not willing to do. A transactional leader may require others to "do as I say," not "do as I do." The transformational leader, by his actions, says "do as I do."

A transformational leader listens, whereas a transactional leader often does a lot of ordering and proclaiming. The type of listening a transformational leader does is empathetic–trying to walk a mile in another's shoes, trying to understand not just what the person is saying but what that person is feeling and experiencing. I often found if a player was underperforming, the best thing I could do was to listen to him, try to find out what was going on in his life. The transactional approach would have been to demote him or criticize him.

Since the need to be understood is very powerful, I often found that if a player was going through a difficult time, my simply making the effort to understand what he was going through served to improve his outlook and his performance. Often I wasn't able to do anything about his problem, but the player knowing I understood and had taken the time to reach out to him seemed to make a real difference.

In order to give our players a voice, we established a Unity Council composed of sixteen players selected from various areas of the team by the players. These players met weekly and brought up any issues they felt might get in the way of team unity. Many of the things they brought to my attention were things that no player would come into my office and complain about. Most of these issues were minor but could grow into bigger problems if not dealt with.

We also let the players set the team goals the last several years I coached. They felt a stronger sense of responsibility for meeting those goals since they were their goals, not mine. This was another area in which we gave them a voice, an opportunity to be heard.

A time during the day in which I did a lot of listening to players was during the twenty to thirty minutes we spent in the weight room after the conclusion of practice. I would lift a few weights with them, but during the time I was there I usually had an informal discussion with four or five players each day about how things were going in their lives. We would discuss academic matters, their families, their high school football team–anything they wanted to talk about. This was on their turf and not a structured situation in which I called them into my office. Over the course of a season I talked to almost every player on several occasions and did a lot of listening. I know they appreciated these opportunities to get better acquainted, and they felt I was hearing their concerns.

A transformational leader seeks to serve the best interests of those he leads. If a key player wants to transfer to another school and this is in the best of interest of that player, the coach does not stand in the way. If a key employee wants to leave the company in order to start his own business, the transformational leader helps him get started, even if that business might later be a competitor.

Lastly, a transformational leader focuses on the process, how things are done, rather than the final outcome. I mentioned earlier how John Wooden started each season by showing his players how to put their socks on so they wouldn't incur blisters, then he moved on to the fundamentals of passing, dribbling, rebounding, yet he never talked about winning. He felt that if the fundamentals were sound, if the practices were precise, if the team chemistry was right, winning would take care of itself.

For John, winning was preparing the best you could possibly prepare. If you did that, even though you might lose on the scoreboard, you had in a real sense won–

because you had done the best you could. I previously mentioned sportswriter Grantland Rice's quote: "For when the One Great Scorer comes to write against your name, it matters not that you won or lost, but how you played the game." Grantland Rice succinctly states the philosophy which is most compatible with transformational leadership; how you play the game is more important than the final outcome.

Over time, adherence to principle, maximum effort, sound fundamentals, and focus on process will more often produce the desired result than an obsession with winning. The longer I coached, the more I began to understand that transformational leadership principles were better for my players, my coaches and the game itself.

Transformational leadership is more conducive to allowing the coach to be a good mentor to his players. A coach who leads by example, cares about each player as a person of great worth regardless of station on the team, listens to his players, emphasizes principles and sound character, stresses solid fundamentals, great effort, and a proper attitude toward opponents and teammates possesses the same qualities which define a good mentor.

In summary, I observed a coach can have very important role in mentoring his players. Players are more impacted by a coach's actions, how he deals with them, and how he lives his life, than by his words alone. If a coach deals with players honestly and keeps promises, then he will be trusted. If a coach is consistent in his treatment of players, win or lose, they will gain confidence in him. If a coach is a good teacher, uses decent language and acts professionally they will gain respect for him. If a coach teaches sound values, and promotes strong character they will appreciate his part in molding their value system, particularly as they move on in their lives. If a coach looks at adversity as an opportunity to learn and to get better, rather than giving up or becoming negative, players will learn a very important life lesson in meeting the difficult challenges they will encounter later in life. A coach who instills strong discipline and a powerful work ethic in his players will have taught them that good things don't come easily, that achievement comes with a price. And finally, by recognizing that the spiritual side of human nature, that which calls us to the best and highest within us, is important and needs to be nurtured just as much as physical and mental preparation, a coach can add a dimension of meaning and purpose which will last a lifetime.

CHAPTER EIGHT
POST-SECONDARY MENTORING

Mentoring is somewhat different for each age group. In elementary school, mentoring often is focused primarily on building trust and offering emotional support. Having love and attention from an adult who has no family or professional obligation to the young person sends the message that the child has value and is worthy of such support. This certainly bolsters a feeling of significance and self-worth in the mentee. Mentors often can be a source of comfort, support and advice. Mentoring at this age often is facilitated by playing board games, exploring topics of interest on the internet, playing catch or shooting baskets while conversing. The mentor can also be of help by ensuring the mentee is mastering the fundamental skills of reading, writing and mathematics. Mentoring is not tutoring, but the mentor can make sure the young person is getting help if basic skills are not being mastered.

During the middle school years mentors often provide a safe harbor and are a source of stability in the sometimes turbulent world of adolescence. Peer pressure, popularity or the lack thereof, hurt feelings and failures as well as successes and accomplishments often need to be talked through and shared. The mentor serves as a sounding board and is also one who can interject an observation or relate a past experience, which gives the young person a better perspective and the realization that he or she is not the only person in the world to have had certain feelings or experiences. The middle school years are particularly challenging as young people are often faced with decisions concerning what they are going to do when pressures to drink, smoke, use drugs, become promiscuous or even join a gang. Having a mentor with whom to talk these things through is invaluable.

The high school years do not offer a clean break from the challenges of middle school. Those decisions concerning lifestyle still loom large and may even be exacerbated by heightened peer pressure. However, it is usually during the high school years that young people begin to think about transitioning into adulthood and preparing for the future. Concerns about grades and whether or not they will be good enough to get into college, what college to attend—or whether going to college is important, are often the focus. For some, the question of whether or not it is important to even graduate from high school is a major consideration.

The decision to drop out of school may seem rather sudden, but such a decision is often the culmination of a series of events over many years. Irregular attendance, lack of engagement in extra-curricular activities at school, not finding relevance in subject matter, substance abuse, peer group influences which discourage academic achievement, can all lead a young person down the path toward dropping out. A mentor can be a powerful antidote to many of these influences which often first appear as early as elementary school. This is why a long-term mentoring relationship can be especially important.

During the high school years the mentor still serves the important function of sounding board, advocate and cheerleader, yet mentoring often takes on the added dimension of coaching the young person through the process of taking the necessary steps to go on to college. Making sure basic college entrance courses are completed, ACT or SAT tests are taken, application papers for college admission are properly filled out, scholarship and financial aid forms are completed and submitted on time, are very important steps with which the mentor can help. Mentors are especially important for potential first generation college students in this regard, as usually no one in their family has experience with the process of gaining admission to a college or university. Many young people don't continue with education beyond high school because they are overwhelmed by the complexity of the process of transitioning to college.

The three stages of mentoring outlined above: elementary, middle school and high school, are all somewhat different, but each stage builds upon the preceding one, and each is very important.

In recent years, we have added a fourth stage of mentoring, mentoring at the post-secondary level. Mentors often work very hard to help their young person through high school graduation and through the college admission process only to find that the mentee completes just a semester or a year of college before leaving school. This is particularly true for first generation college students. First generation college students often lack a frame of reference regarding the demands of college life. Therefore, they look to a mentor when a roommate is difficult to deal with, when they realize they are in the wrong major field of study, or when the college experience and being away from home simply seems overwhelming.

Prior to implementing post secondary mentoring opportunities, sixty percent of TeamMates first generation college students enrolled for their second year. Once we provided those first generation college students with a post secondary mentor, however, the percentage continuing on with the second year increased to more than ninety percent, a huge improvement. Providing first generation college students with a mentor increased the number of students continuing their education beyond the first year by one third. Once a student gets through the first year of college and goes on to the second, there is a great likelihood they will complete their college degree.

I recall talking to one of the young men who played football for me at the University of Nebraska several years ago. This young man was from an inner-city environment and his parents had never gone to college. His roommate was from a more afflu-ent background, and the roommate's parents were college grad-uates. The young man whose parents had not gone to college recounted how his roommate's parents called at least twice a week to ask how a certain test had gone, how a term paper was progressing, how he was getting along with a professor, while he never had a conversation with his parents during his college years which related to any of those topics. He had good parents and they cared about him; they just had no frame of reference when it came to doing college work. I could tell he missed the support his roommate received from home. Fortunately he ben-efited from coaches and academic counselors who offered advice and encouragement to him, but many first generation college students don't have the support an athletic department provides.

A post-secondary mentor is one who has graduated from college and is able to relate to the challenges most students face in higher education. Such a mentor can refer the student to resources on campus that can be helpful in dealing with personal problems and can provide advice concerning majors, intern-ships, work-study opportunities, scholarships, and summer employment and career advice beyond college. A post-sec-ondary mentor is able to serve as an example of one who has been able to work through all of the challenges of college and complete a degree. Above all, a post-secondary mentor is an encourager and a support person.

One post-secondary mentee summarized her experience with TeamMates as follows:

"Having a post-secondary mentor has been the greatest thing for me. I joined the program when I was in sixth grade (eight years ago!) and have loved it ever since. I was worried once I graduated I wouldn't have that kind of support anymore, but I was wrong. I was fortunate enough to receive another mentor that I have formed an incredible bond with. Being away from home, like many students in post-secondary education, having mentor support you is a wonderful thing. I know I couldn't have done it without my mentor's support. It is nice to have somebody to believe in you when you don't believe in yourself. My college career would have been very different without my post-secondary mentor."

Post-secondary mentoring is different than mentoring at the elementary, middle school and high school levels. The post-secondary mentor may not be located in the same community in which the student attends college, so seeing the mentee on a weekly basis in the school setting is often impossible. Our mentors typically meet inperson with their post-secondary mentee an average of once per month but communicate regularly by telephone, email or social media on a weekly, and sometimes almost daily, basis. If the mentor is located in the mentee's home community a face-to-face meeting is possible when the student returns home for a weekend or a vacation period. If the mentor does, happen to be in the community where the mentee attends school it is much easier to maintain a reasonable amount of personal, face-to-face contact.

Benefits to the mentee are varied. One post-secondary mentor wrote this about her mentee: "I promoted a community-based after-school program to her during her first year, since she was an education major. The position has allowed her opportunities to work with children in an educational setting and network with teachers. Additionally, I was able to help her narrow her choices for a study abroad program. She is now in Europe, learning a foreign language and growing tremendously in confidence and independence."

Another post-secondary mentor said: "As a person wanting to pursue a career in medicine, he has benefited greatly from the scholarships he has received through TeamMates. In addition he recently received a new laptop computer."

A post-secondary mentee said, "This experience makes me want to become a better person and strive for more than I would have before having a mentor." I think what she was saying is that having a person love you and invest in you often makes the recipient of that love and nurturing desire to respond to their better impulses and not disappoint the one who has invested in them.

A post-secondary mentor mentioned she was able to help reduce her mentee's financial stress, "I have helped her find employment and additional sources of funding for school.

A post-secondary mentee commented, "Having a mentor so close has given me a strong foundation in regards to career advice and graduate school preparation. It is comforting to know I have a trustful resource in my mentor whenever I am questioning myself, seeking advice, or needing a second opinion on any step throughout my college pathway." Sometimes it is important to have affirmation that one is deciding correctly with regard to choosing a major or a career path. In working with college students for many years, I often saw athletes change majors multiple times, each time prolonging their education. There are so many options confronting today's college student that it is easy to second-guess decisions and suffer "paralysis from analysis." A mentor can often help a young person think through options and concentrate on strengths, which helps clarify educational goals.

Mentors can be very helpful in guiding their mentees progress toward specific career objectives. One mentor reported,

"My mentee wanted to break the cycle of poverty he has known all his life. He sees the best avenue to realize his goal is through entrepreneurial activities. Working with our friends at Gallup, my mentee took the Entrepreneurial StrengthsFinder Profile, and then we spent several hours sitting with the people at Gallup who developed this tool, discussing his strengths and challenges as a successful entrepreneur." This mentor was a valuable resource in getting his mentee introduced to people who could be of great help in developing entrepreneurial skills.

Another mentor was able to provide valuable insight regarding internships in the business world. "As we discussed his goals for the future he asked if I knew of any internship opportunities in Omaha. I gave a few leads and encouraged him to review what he found and get back to me. He researched, and we prioritized his list. I helped him get an interview, and he blew them away. He started as a part-time intern in their finance department and has a full time internship with them this summer."

Transitioning from a small town, rural setting to a large university can be particularly daunting. "The past two years have provided a "win-win" experience for both my mentee and for me. My mentee successfully transitioned from a rural area into the University of Nebraska-Lincoln. Postsecondary mentoring has given me the opportunity to share some of the learning I acquired many years ago when I transitioned from a small town into a university." Having a mentor who could draw upon past experience to help steer a young person through the complexities of a large institution was undoubtedly very helpful in this instance.

Sometimes students are inherently shy and lack self-confidence. Attending a larger institution where it is easy to assume everyone else is brighter and more talented can be a very difficult adjustment. A mentor wrote: "When I first met (my mentee) she was timid, nervous and worried about classes, making friends and surviving the adjustment to college life. I struggled to find ways to encourage and help her at the beginning, but as our friendship grew so did her self-confidence. She settled into a new routine. She chose a major to fit her interests. She learned to be an independent adult. She mentioned that I helped her get through some of the early challenges of college. It's been a pleasure to witness her growth over the past three years."

Some students don't see higher education as an option. A first generation college student, now a sophomore at the University of Nebraska Lincoln, wrote: "As a first generation Hispanic student, I witnessed many doors shut in front of me…to the point that receiving higher education seemed like a farfetched idea. With the help of my amazing mentor encouraging me along the way to keep working hard and not give up. It was her hard work week after week, and scholarship essay after scholarship application that a door finally opened and here I am one step closer!"

A mentee commented on the advantage of having her high school mentor continue as her mentor during her college years. "My mentor has been more than just a mentor to me. I am so blessed to have our friendship to continue on through college. Whenever I have a problem or need advice, she is the first person I will think of. She will be honest with me and tell me what I need to hear. Not only will she help me figure out my problem, she gives me the opportunity to make my own choice as well, but will support me no matter what. . . . My mentor is a part of who I am, and if she was gone, so would be a piece of me. I never met someone who cared more about me than my mentor. . . .This program has given me even more than just a vision, purpose, and hope. It has filled the missing piece I have had all my life. It has motivated me even more to do better and to give back. It has given me a life that I have never imagined at a young age." This young lady has achieved at a high level with the help of her mentor who has filled a large void in her life. This mentor has told her mentee what the mentee needs to hear, yet has also given the mentee the freedom to make her own choices and to deal with the consequences. This mentor is very wise and has clearly been very important to the young college student she is now mentoring.

Mentors often mention that they themselves have learned a good deal through the mentoring process. One mentor wrote about how his mentoring experience changed some misperceptions: "Our relationship has renewed my confidence in our society's' future as it relates to young black men. Most of what you see and hear in the media regarding race relations and crime would have one believe this population does not embrace our societies' values. Our frank discussions regarding this perception has been very beneficial for me. . . . I have had to step back and try to put myself in his place as a 20 year old black man. Not an easy task but a very revealing effort for me."

Mentoring serves as an opportunity to learn a great deal about the challenges some young people face. This mentor, who has enjoyed a great deal of success in the business world, wrote about her experience with a college student who came from a very different background. "Meeting with my mentee for the first time was eye-opening. I grew up in a small town and lived a very sheltered life. . . .When you grow up that way you tend to think that everyone is like you. You start to believe that your 'reality' is the reality that everyone else experiences. Nothing could be further from the truth. My mentee has had many obstacles to overcome. . . . My mentee is the first person in her family to attend college. She understands what a privilege it is to attend college whereas many of us took it for granted. My mentee's success is tenuous but she is hungry for an education and determined to succeed. Getting to know this young woman has been a huge wake-up call for me. . . . I have seen for the first time what a difference just one person can make if they are willing to step forward and spend a few hours a month with someone."

A mentor who runs a large business said, "I have a new relationship that has provided me with an experience with someone who is faced with a different set of challenges vs. what I experience every day in my job. I would like to think I am a better listener and have tried to make sure my thoughts have been constructive and not critical." This mentor has learned what so many mentors report. They have learned how important it is to listen, to experience life through another's eyes. We often hear about the difficult circumstances of others, but it often doesn't fully hit home until we sit face to face with someone going through those struggles.

There is great satisfaction in seeing persistence pay off. "I feel energized when I meet with my mentee. I know he is really happy to see me. We went through about a year where he avoided me. I feel I am personally helping him thru this process which is very gratifying to me," says one mentor.

Another mentor saw the value of persistence when he was asked by his post-secondary mentee, whom he had mentored through junior high school and high school, if he would also mentor his younger brother. "You can't get a better recommendation than that, I thought. Even after seven years with my mentee that was the first real time it came to me that we were having an impact. I guess I had thought I was just making small talk when we were together, but now I believe he was actually listening and making mental notes. . . . Mentoring for the last several years has been rewarding in ways only a few can understand. There is no compensation that could outweigh my hopes that my mentee continues his creative path and emerges as the person that he has the ability to become."

Since post-secondary mentoring involves a mentee with more maturity, mentors often report they now have someone in their life who is more than a mentee; they now have a real friend who is on a more equal footing with them. A post-secondary mentor recently reported, "I wanted to get some ideas from her on a theme for Leadership Summit since her major is now including Event Planning. She was the student director for the Wizard of Oz her senior year in high school and shared with me some of her ideas for that theme. Therefore that became our theme this year for our conference. . . . Mentoring post-secondary is such a different level of friendship. We communicate more on an adult to adult basis, still keeping the same love for each other that was built from her younger years...Now we are more on an equal level, adult friend to adult friend. It's been pure joy!"

A final observation from a mentor reflects what most post-secondary mentors say in one way or another. "My mentee is very active as a freshman. She is a very smart and beautiful young woman inside and out, and watching her bloom and encouraging her to go even further than she thought she could go is so rewarding." There is great satisfaction in seeing a young person mature and grow into a productive adult, which even they often had no idea they were capable of becoming. Knowing one is part of that process as a mentor is very rewarding. There is no question that mentoring, be it at the elementary, middle school, high school or post-secondary level, adds a significant element of meaning, purpose and significance to the mentor's life. Giving one's time, wisdom and love to another person who is not in a position to give something in return is, paradoxically, one of the greatest gifts a person can receive. The mentor receives a gift in return which is priceless, the gift of greater meaning and purpose in one's life.

CHAPTER NINE

INFORMAL MENTORING

Most of the focus of this book has been on formal mentoring, mentoring which is structured and intentional. However, most mentoring is informal and not structured. Research by The National Mentoring Partnership indicates there are 46 million young people in the United States between eight and eighteen years of age. Of the 46 million young people of prime mentoring age, 6.9 million are in structured mentoring programs such as TeamMates and Big Brothers Big Sisters. Another 23.1 million young people in the eight to eighteen age group report having had a mentoring relationship outside of a formal mentoring program. The mentor might have been a close friend or relative, a teacher, a coach, a scoutmaster or anyone who cared enough about the young person to invest time and caring in the child's life.

The remaining 16 million of the total 46 million reported they never had someone in their life they would call a mentor. So about one third had no mentor, about one in seven have been in a formal mentoring program and nearly one half have had an informal mentoring relationship of some kind.

A study done by the White House Council For Community Solutions in 2012 found that eighty percent of young people between the ages of sixteen and twenty four who were no longer in school and were unemployed wanted a mentor in their lives. They needed someone to show them the way out of their difficult circumstances. The study indicates there are approximately

6.7 million of these disconnected youth. They cost society roughly $93 billion dollars each year because of lost productivity and related social costs. It is safe to say the great majority of these young people have not been in a formal mentoring program and have also not had an informal mentor. If they had a mentor earlier in their lives, they would be much less likely to be unemployed high school dropouts.

Informal mentoring is difficult to define because so much of what constitutes informal mentoring is in the eyes of the person being mentored. What one person would describe as a mentoring relationship would not be interpreted as mentoring by another. However, there is no doubt that much of what is perceived as mentoring is of an informal nature. We have already examined coaching as a form of mentoring, and this would likely fall under the heading of informal mentoring, yet there are strong overtones of formal mentoring as well. The coach has a position of authority, the athlete is expected to attend practices, behave in certain ways and adhere to team rules. There is little optional behavior on an athletic team, whereas in most informal mentoring there is a great deal of discretion the mentee has as to whether to engage with the mentor or not.

I will devote this chapter to informal mentors who have been very important in my life and also describe some informal mentoring opportunities I have had.

My Father

My father was a significant mentor to me. I have already described his being overseas for nearly five years during World War II and the impact his absence had on my life. Fortunately, my uncle served as a mentor and role model during the time my dad was gone. When he came home, my dad was pretty much a stranger in that I had been four years old when he left and was nine when he returned. I had very few memories of him. I wanted to please him, and there is no question that he was a major influence on me during the next several years.

There were five critical attributes my dad instilled in me. First was a love of athletic competition. Since I ended up spending most of my life either as an athlete or a coach, this was obviously a powerful theme. We lived across the street from Hastings College, and my dad and I never missed a game there. Hastings High School played football at the college field, and we attended those games as well. He often attended practices. We played catch with the football and baseball, and he went to all of my athletic events from midget baseball on up. He never pushed too hard or had unrealistic expectations, but his love of athletics was contagious and dominated much of my life.

Second, my dad insisted if I was going to do a job that I do it well and work hard. He had me taking care of lawns with a push mower when I was ten or eleven, shoveling sidewalks and later working on the wash rack at his automobile dealership, where it took about an hour to wash a car according to his specifications. There was not to be a speck of dirt on the car, inside or out, by the time I was done. Later I worked on construction crews in the summer to put myself through college. He made sure I knew what it was to do difficult physical work and to do a thorough job, and that stayed with me as time went on.

Third, my dad was the son of a Presbyterian minister and he made sure our family was in church and Sunday School every week. He didn't just send my brother and me; he and my mother were always there as well. As the son of a preacher he fought hard against appearing pious and tried to be seen as a regular guy with a good sense of humor, but his example concerning going to church as a family was a major influence. My faith became a very important part of my life.

Fourth, he loved history, particularly the history of the

American West. He read a history book of some type almost every evening and had several rare books. He was an expert on the early settlers, the fur trade, the Oregon Trail, the Mormon Trail, Lewis and Clark, the homesteaders. He also was very knowledgeable about the Civil War and World War II. All of this probably had something to do with my being a history major in college and enjoying history. We urged him to write a book, but he always said he was afraid that he would write something that wouldn't be good enough.

His final influence came during his later years. I wrote earlier about my dad going back to Europe to retrace the path which his unit took through France, Belgium and Germany during World War II and how it affected my mother emotionally. It seemed to her that he was leaving for war again. She suffered a major stroke while he was gone, and I had to call him in Paris in the middle of the night to tell him to come home, that mom was seriously ill. She survived the stroke but could no longer walk or speak. My dad had a major heart attack a few years before and wasn't in the best of health, but he insisted on taking care of her as best he could. He would often get up to tend to her needs during the night and his looking after her probably hastened his own demise from another heart attack. His devotion to my mother through some very difficult years has left a lasting impression on me concerning what marriage, devotion and servanthood are all about.

Bob Devaney

Having never coached before arriving at the University of Nebraska in 1962, much of what I learned about coaching was from the person I worked for the next thirty two years, Bob Devaney.

Bob didn't have an easy life. His father worked on the ore

boats on the Great Lakes during the Great Depression. Bob worked in a foundry for a time and then decided there might be a better way to earn a living. He enrolled at Alma College, played football there and graduated in 1939. He was a high school coach at several small high schools in Michigan. His last high school job was at Alpena, when he got a big break. He was hired as an assistant football coach at Michigan State and worked for Coach Biggie Munn and later for Coach Duffy Daugherty. Duffy recommended Bob to people at the University of Wyoming, who were looking for a head coach at the time, and Bob did an outstanding job at Wyoming from 1957 through the 1961 season.

The University of Nebraska had endured twenty consecutive seasons of rather dismal football performances, having had only two winning seasons during that time and winning no championships prior to hiring Bob Devaney. Bob and I arrived at the University of Nebraska at approximately the same time, January of 1962. I had opted not to return to the Washington Redskins due to a chronic hamstring injury and decided I would go to graduate school in educational psychology with an eye toward college administration work.

I knew I would miss football so I contacted Bob and asked him if he could use any help from me as a graduate assistant coach. He said he didn't need coaches, but he understood some football players needed supervision in their wing of Selleck Quadrangle, and he said he would provide meals at the training table if I would move into Selleck and keep the players on track. When spring football started he did let me do some coaching, and I was a graduate assistant for the next few years as well as a graduate student and teacher in the Educational Psychology Department.

I met Nancy Tederman shortly after coming to the University of Nebraska and married her that same August, so 1962 was a very big year. She was planning to teach in California and had signed a contract to do so. I'm glad she said yes to my proposal.

Once I had completed my graduate work and was set to move into the academic world, I found that football had too great a pull on my life. I went to see Bob and told him I wanted to coach. Bob hired me as a receiver and quarterback coach. I told him I could get a job in academics for $10,000 a year and asked him to pay me that amount. He agreed; our process was much different than negotiating coaches' salaries today.

I had a first-hand view of a remarkable turnaround in Nebraska's football fortunes. Bob took a team which had finished 3-6-1 the year before he arrived and went 9-2 in 1962 with largely the same group of players. He followed that season, which had Nebraskans in shock, with four consecutive Big Eight championships and major bowl appearances. Two of those bowl games had national championship possibilities. Next came a couple of 6-4 seasons, which were accompanied by some grumbling by the fans, but those years were followed by 9-2, 12-0-1, 13-0 and 9-2-1 years in which Nebraska won conference championships and the 1970 and 1971 National Championships. Bob was unbelievably popular. Nebraska now had a prominent place in the world of college football.

I had played under several coaches and had an idea of what made a good coach versus a poor coach, but I had never been a coach before the 1962 season at the University of Nebraska. Since Bob Devaney was the only head coach I had coached under, he was a mentor to me in terms of providing insight into what coaching was all about.

I didn't plan to be a coach when I returned to Nebraska, but I still watched Bob closely. Since I had a front row seat to the remarkable turnaround in Nebraska's football fortunes I was able to observe those things Bob did that seemed to contribute to the transformation.

The first thing that struck me about Bob was his sense of humor. He had a keen Irish wit and a good sense of timing in how and when to use it. He had a temper and would occasionally lay into players, but he didn't stay angry and by the end of practice he would tell a joke or two, kid the player he had chewed out during practice and leave the field with people feeling good.

The fans loved his stories, many of which he told over and over, but people still enjoyed them immensely. If we lost a game he was more entertaining than ever, but he also knew the laughter would end fairly quickly if we lost very often. So Bob made football fun—at least more so than what the players and fans had experienced for the previous twenty years.

Second, Bob's practices were well organized and adhered to a strict time schedule—no practice lasted longer than two hours. Nobody stood around, things moved crisply, and yet Bob was good about limiting the amount of full contact the players had during the week's preparation. We had some hitting on Tuesday and Wednesday, but not for very long, Thursday was a practice in sweat clothes and Friday was short and also without pads. By Saturday afternoon players were ready to fly around and play with great energy. The previous coaching staff had been known for long practices, up to four hours long at times, and a penchant for full scale scrimmages. The players appreciated the change in practice routine; the body can withstand only so many "train wrecks" before there is a decline in performance.

Third, Bob's teams had an identity. He believed football was a tough, physical sport and wanted players who played the game that way. Bob did some fighting, both in the ring and out of it, back in his youth in Saginaw, Michigan, and that mentality stayed with him during his coaching career. Opposing teams knew they were in for a long afternoon when they played Nebraska, as Bob's teams would hit hard and not back off. They came to play and play aggressively. Bob's mindset was part of the physical nature of his teams. I don't believe he ever went into a game he didn't think he would win. Occasionally I have seen coaches play ultra-conservatively so they would not get beaten badly, but they had already conceded any chance for victory. Bob wasn't cut from that cloth.

Fourth, Bob was exceptionally loyal. I saw this demonstrated following the 1968 football season. This was Bob's "worst" season at Nebraska. We wound up 6-4, a winning record, but we lost to Kansas State 12-0 in Lincoln and lost to Oklahoma 47-0 in Norman, the last game of the season. The fans were very unhappy, and the press was not sympathetic. In the 1940s and 1950s a 6-4 season would have looked pretty good, but not now, not after several consecutive conference championships.

A few folks were calling for Bob's job, but many more wanted Bob to fire some assistants and replace them with new blood. Bob came out swinging in reply to such talk and let be known that "if one coach went, we all went." That pretty much ended any conversation about firing assistants. As a 31 year old with a wife and three young children, I can assure you I appreciated Bob's loyalty and learned a good deal in the process.

When any of Bob's assistants got to the age where coaching was too demanding, he found other jobs in the Athletic Department for them—something he could do as Athletic Director. He was also very loyal to former players and his friends. Because of that loyalty, the athletic department at Nebraska was a place where people didn't spend a lot of time looking over their shoulder wondering when they might be replaced. They knew it was important to perform well, but they also felt appreciated and valued. It was a good place to work.

Fifth, Bob was not a micro-manager. He gave his assistant football coaches and the head coaches who worked under him while he was athletic director an area of responsibility and expected them to do their job. He would not interfere with a drill in practice as some head coaches would do. As a football coach he would not criticize an assistant coach in front of his players. As Athletic Director he did not criticize his head coaches and leave them dangling, subject to speculation about when they might be fired.

It is extremely rare for a former head coach, especially one who has been highly successful, to not meddle in the sport he once coached after he becomes Athletic Director. Bob never interfered with the way I coached the football team. He was supportive; the door to his office was always open, he visited the locker room after every game, and, along with his friend Bob Logsdon, brought dinner to the football coaching staff every Sunday evening while we were working late. He never told me to run a specific play or play a certain player, and I don't recall Bob and I ever having a major disagreement. It was very helpful to have an athletic director who knew what it was like to be booed by the fans, have his starting quarterback lost for the season to injury or lose a game because of an odd bounce of the football. There aren't many athletic directors like that. I was very fortunate to have had one.

Finally, Bob was willing to change and take chances. He had used an unbalanced line, full-house backfield at Wyoming and in his early years at Nebraska (similar to what he had learned at Michigan State under Duffy Daugherty). This worked well for a time, but then we had two back to back 6-4 seasons, and, along with those seasons, the fans' displeasure. Bob asked me to overhaul the offense for the 1969 season, and Monte Kiffen also made changes to the defense. Both Monte and I had come up through the graduate assistant ranks and were new kids on the block as far as the older assistants were concerned, so Bob was taking a pretty big gamble on both of us.

He also gave approval to our starting a strength and conditioning program run by Boyd Epley, a former pole vaulter at Nebraska who had gotten into body building. Since strength training is a staple of every athletic program today, it sounds odd that this was an innovative move on Bob's part. However, traditional wisdom at the time was that weight lifting made you "muscle bound" and would decrease speed and athleticism. Having been in the coaching profession for many years, Bob shared many of those views, but he was willing to give Boyd a chance, and Boyd became the first full-time strength coach in intercollegiate athletics.

So we went from the unbalanced line offense to the I-formation, changed exclusively to a 5-2 defense, and initiated a comprehensive strength and conditioning program. The results weren't immediately gratifying, as we began the 1969 season 2-2, but we kept getting better and won the rest, beating Oklahoma 44-14 in the last regular season game (quite a turn-around from the thumping we endured the year before) and then finished up by beating Georgia soundly in the Sun Bowl. That 9-2 season was the foundation for two consecutive undefeated National Championship teams in 1970 and 1971. Suddenly we were smarter coaches, and there was no more talk of firing.

Bob took another big chance in naming me as the head football coach in 1973. I was 35 years old and many doubted the wisdom of that move. I was young, had no previous head coaching experience at any level and had only coached at Nebraska. I had not even had the official title of offensive coordinator, although I had fulfilled that function for the previous four seasons. Bob's support and confidence in me was very important and much appreciated.

Even though Bob Devaney and I were very different people and had different lifestyles, I consider him to be an important mentor in my life. I benefited not just from his support professionally but also from the example he set in how to treat people in a way that brought out the best in them.

Woody Varner

I had four informal mentors during my life. I have mentioned my uncle Virgil who took me under his wing when my dad was gone during WWII, my dad, Bob Devaney, and the fourth was D.B. "Woody" Varner, Chancellor and President of the University of Nebraska from 1970-1976. Woody came from Cottonwood, Texas, hence his nickname, and attended Texas A&M University where he was a varsity basketball player.

Woody went into academic administration work, serving as an administrator at Michigan State and then becoming President of Oakland University, also in Michigan, before being hired at the University of Nebraska. Woody and his wife Paula soon became Nebraska football fans and, for some reason, seemed to take a liking to me as a young assistant football coach. That supportive attitude continued after I became the head coach in 1973.

Those first few years as head coach were difficult. We won quite a few games, going 9-2-1 in 1973, followed by 9-3, 10-2, 9-3-1, and 9-3 seasons. We went to bowl games each one of those years; among those were the Cotton, Sugar and Fiesta bowls. We tied for the Big Eight championship in the 10-2, 1975 season, but there was one major problem—we lost to Oklahoma each of my first five seasons. As far as most fans were concerned, it had become a one-game season; if we didn't beat Oklahoma it was a bad year.

After a tough loss, Bob Devaney, as head football coach, would still go to the American Legion Club, have dinner and socialize into the wee hours. When I was head coach and we lost, I went home and took the phone off the hook, as people would call to vent their frustration. I then contemplated the fact that I probably wouldn't be the football coach at the University of Nebraska much longer if things didn't change fairly quickly.

On those bleak post-Oklahoma game November evenings there would be a knock on the door. I would look through the window to see if it was a friend or foe, and it would be Woody and Paula Varner. Not many football coaches would be visited by the President of the University and his wife after a game, especially after a big loss. They would sit down in our living room and make small talk. Woody had a great sense of humor and would soon elicit a smile or two, then a laugh, when I thought that I would never smile or laugh again. Losing is a little bit like dying, only you had to live with a loss to Oklahoma for the next year, and dying puts an end to the misery.

Woody was a very kind man. He and Paula cared enough to spend time with Nancy, me and our children when very few people wanted to be around us. There were undoubtedly many post-game obligations with boosters and alumni they could have attended rather than maintaining a vigil with a young football coach and his family.

Woody was an exceptional public speaker. He never used notes, weaving his thoughts together seamlessly and without effort, and always laced with a wonderful sense of humor. He was a great fundraiser and later became the head of the University of Nebraska Foundation. Because of his engaging personality and his wit, he could get people to donate to the University and enjoy doing it.

He was a true Renaissance man. He loved the performing arts and built a beautiful performing arts center on the campus. He was an avid gardener and took great pride in his horticultural skills. He loved athletics. He was a very devoted family man.

I learned from Woody that the gift of time, particularly when things are bleak, is the greatest gift of all. Woody took time to be with people even though he had many pressing responsibilities. He was always fun to be around; his sense of humor and his diverse interests made him a great source of encouragement and companionship.

I was very fortunate to have the friendship and support of the Athletic Director and the University President, not just nominal support, but a genuine personal supportive friendship, upon which I could count. Very few coaches are that lucky.

And so, even though I was never in a formal mentoring relationship, I benefited from a wonderful group of mentors that influenced and shaped me. I knew it was important to be my own person; it would be a mistake to try to coach exactly like Bob Devaney or try to be another Woody Varner. However, I was able to take several things from each one of those mentoring relationships which were of great value.

I have written about my grandfather, Thomas C. Osborne. Even though I did not get to know him well because of his living several hundred miles away and his death when I was nine years old, my mental image of who he was and what he stood for was a powerful influence in my life. I wanted to live my life in a way that would make him proud. In that sense he was a mentor even after his death.

John Wooden, through his books and a few personal interactions, also was an important informal mentor. Like Bob Devaney, he impacted how I approached my coaching career. Mentoring can occur at a distance and with little interpersonal contact.

While I am reflecting on past relationships, it would be wrong not to mention my mother. She was a school teacher, but when she married my dad, as was customary at that time, she quit work and became a full-time homemaker. When I came along she gave me her undivided attention as my dad traveled the state of Nebraska Monday through Friday and was home only on the weekends. She taught me to read when I was three, and, as is often the case with an older child, placed a good deal of responsibility on me. She had confidence I could succeed at whatever she asked me to do, and I think her confidence rubbed off on me. Her family was the focus of her life, and we knew her devotion to us would never waver.

As I think about the foundation I received from my family and the mentors I have had, I would have to say I have been extremely fortunate. Many young people are growing up today with relatively little family support and can't point to a single mentoring relationship, formal or informal, that they have had. As I have mentioned, having approximately one third of our young people grow up without a significant mentor, and often without stable families as well, is quite likely the greatest threat our nation faces today.

I have benefited from the influence of some excellent informal mentors, and have also enjoyed the role of being a mentor in informal mentoring relationships. Having coached approximately two thousand young men in my coaching career, I often hear from former players who want to talk and reflect on things that happened during their playing days which now have more significance to them with the passage of time. They want to talk, sometimes they seek advice, often they simply want to renew our relationship. In many cases they are seeking a mentor.

Two informal mentoring experiences I have had lately are worth relating. One of them has been with a former player, the other with a complete stranger.

The first instance involves a young man we recruited from Texas in the early 1980s, Ricky Simmons. I have not used the names of mentors or mentees previously to protect their identities. Ricky is an exception because he asked me to mention him by name. Ricky had exceptional speed and played wide receiver. He had a solid family, his father was a school administrator and his mother was a teacher. He had several scholarship offers coming out of high school and was leaning toward the University of Oklahoma, but his parents told him he was going to Nebraska because they liked our academic program and felt good about the culture at Nebraska. Ricky played well and started for two of our finest teams in 1982 and 1983. Both teams went 12-1, with the 1983 team losing by one point to Miami in a national championship game.

Ricky was drafted in the NFL, had some money and celebrity, and drifted into a drug addiction which became very expensive, exhausted his financial resources, and eventually ended his football career. Things went downhill from there, and he had several prison stays. We lost contact for many years and then I heard that he was in the Tecumseh, Nebraska, prison and really struggling. I wrote him a very simple, brief letter letting him know I cared about him and still believed in him. He reports that the letter, simple as it was, had a powerful impact on him, and he dropped to his knees and turned his life over to Christ after reading it.

I believe the letter impacted him as it did for several reasons. His parents had died, and he thought there was nobody left who cared about him. He knew from our previous coach-player relationship that he could trust me, and he knew I cared about him. Also he was at a time and place in his life where he had run out of options and turning his life over to Jesus was the only thing which made any sense to him.

Whatever the reasons, Ricky made a dramatic turnaround which was more than a temporary "jailhouse conversion." Upon his release from prison he stayed on track, became a licensed substance abuse counselor and stayed true to his faith. He gets up at 3:00 a.m. each morning and spends time in the scriptures and in prayer. He has a speaking schedule in which he addresses high school assemblies, church groups, service clubs and other organizations. He also does individual substance abuse counseling. He is articulate and speaks from considerable experience, which captures and holds the attention of those he addresses. Unfortunately that experience was obtained at a great price.

The reason I refer to this relationship as a mentoring relationship is that Ricky comes to see me once a week, without fail.
The visits aren't long, just a way of staying in touch and, I think,
a point of accountability for him. By seeing me once a week, he
is reminded of the changes he has made in his life and his need
to stay true to his commitment to abstain from harmful sub-
stances and also stay true to his faith. I am proud of what he is
doing, and I am glad I can play a small part in his life.

A second informal mentoring relationship involves a young
man who, as a complete stranger, contacted me out of the blue
approximately a year and a half ago and asked if I would be his
mentor. I told him I would meet with him and would consider
being his mentor, but I needed to know more about him. I was
impressed by the fact that he had gone to considerable trouble
in contacting me as I had left the Athletic Department at the
University, and he had shown a great deal of perseverance in
locating me.

He called and said he had written a book about leadership
and wanted me to read it. I was catching a flight out of Omaha
that morning and told him if he could meet me at the airport I
would read his book. He arrived at the airport, out of breath, just
as I was about to pass through security and handed the book to
me. I read it on the flight and found it was a well written book
about servant leadership. He told me later he had based much of
his book on some notes I had given to his brother and other
coaches when I had spoken about servant leadership at
Creighton University some time before. I could tell from reading
it he was intelligent, and I was impressed by the effort he made
to deliver the book to me, so I agreed to be his mentor.

When we first met, I found this young man lived in North
Omaha and had an interesting story to tell. After graduating
from Omaha Benson High School he had enrolled at a small
college, did poorly academically, was dismissed, gained re-entry

and left school again. Even though his college career did not appear to lead to anything positive, he did take one thing away from his time there. A faculty member had told him he possessed leadership skills. This small piece of affirmation led him to see himself differently and caused him to become interested in the subject of leadership.

He told me that while in college he had been a drug dealer and a gang member. Sharing this information with me was not a very good way to convince me I should be his mentor, but I did appreciate his honesty. He went on to say that at one point after leaving college he was at a party and reflected on the fact that his life was going nowhere. He reports he began to weep about his circumstances and decided to go home and talk to his father. He was fortunate to have a father, one who cared for him, and apparently they talked for the rest of the night. The reflection on the direction in which his life was headed, coupled with the love and advice he received from his father, was a turning point in his life.

He started and pastored a church, developed a mentoring program to serve troubled young people, and taught classes on leadership and entrepreneurship—quite a change from selling drugs. Most of the people in his church and his entrepreneurial and leadership classes were from North Omaha, an area of the city which was struggling financially and had high unemployment and crime levels. He also introduced me to his wife and child. I could tell he was a dedicated husband and father and he desired to make life better for people, particularly the people of North Omaha.

After we met several times and I got to know more about all he was attempting to do, it became apparent he was spread very thin. His church had about 80 members, his mentoring program had approximately 90 matches, and he had a good number of students in his entrepreneurial classes he was trying to assist with their start-up businesses. He was having difficulty finding places for his church members to meet, and the church was struggling financially. The logistics of running a mentoring program were overwhelming. In addition he also was having difficulty locating a place to teach his entrepreneurial classes.

I asked him which of these projects he was most passionate about and had him think about where he might do the most good for his community. We talked about the fact he was doing so many things that it would be very hard to do any of them very well. Eventually he came to decide his main passion was that of helping people start businesses and create jobs. Small business ownership was lacking in North Omaha, the economy was suffering, and unemployment was a major problem.

Even though it was difficult, he decided to give up his church and his mentoring program and focus on teaching people entrepreneurial skills. He taught them how to develop an idea into a business proposal, how to write a business plan, how to access capital to start a business, and how to learn from other business leaders. I connected him with the president of Metro Community College, and the president was able to find class space for him and eventually work his classes into the curriculum. He is developing a track record of having helped start a number of successful businesses in the community. He has also helped many existing businesses become more profitable.

He has plans to build a small business incubation center where people can come to develop their business ideas and gain valuable insight from others. He has been written about in newspapers and also an entrepreneur magazine. He is mentioned as an example of what can be done in other cities which are struggling financially.

This does not mean there will not be problems ahead. He is still in the beginning stages of what he wants to accomplish, but he has come a long way and has the potential to do a great deal of good in his community.

He indicates the things which have been most beneficial to him from our relationship include the following:

He said that lacked confidence in himself; he had struggled with this lack of confidence throughout his life. He felt my willingness to meet with him and show I believed in him was very important to his being able to move forward and accomplish all that he has done. It gave his confidence a boost at the right time.

Secondly, he indicated that through our conversations he was able to sort out what his main mission needed to be. He knew he was spread very thin, but he didn't know what he needed to focus on, what his area of greatest strength was, until we spent time talking through all he was trying to do.

Not long ago I met with a very successful businessman who was well known for his entrepreneurial skills, and he asked about the young man I had been mentoring. I was surprised we had this common acquaintance. The businessman indicated the person I had been mentoring had called him and asked if the businessman would also serve as his mentor. So the young man I had mentored had learned something. He realized that others could be of help, and he was not shy about asking for their assistance. He sensed that learning from someone who was a successful entrepreneur (which I wasn't) could provide him with additional skills and insights.

I mentioned I have been extremely fortunate to have the informal mentors I have had in my life. All of those mentors came into my life without my asking them. Sometimes it is important to seek a mentor if you are looking for a particular kind of guidance or want to engage with a specific person. Having the courage and initiative to make things happen, such as the young man mentioned here, is very important. Many people are not lucky enough to have the right person come along at the right time, so finding a good mentor can make all the difference.

CHAPTER TEN

EFFECTIVE MENTORING PRACTICES

As mentioned previously, I have been very fortunate to have had excellent informal mentors. However, most of my involvement in the mentoring field has been in the area of formal mentoring through the TeamMates Mentoring Program. Over the past twenty four years, we have learned a great deal about mentoring as we have provided services to several thousand young people.

Our model has been entirely school-based, with nearly all of our mentoring done in the school setting. We believe school-based mentoring is particularly effective for six reasons:

First, since mentoring is done in the school setting there are fewer concerns about the safety of the mentee or mentor. There is less chance of something inappropriate happening or being misunderstood in a school setting.

Second, the mentor is in the vicinity of teachers, counselors and administrators and can get a more accurate picture of what is going on in the life of the mentee through occasional interaction with those who work with the young person on a daily basis. Mentoring is not tutoring, but the mentor can usually see to it that the mentee gets the academic help needed through school personnel.

Third, the mentor is able to observe how the mentee interacts with other students at times and is often more aware of interpersonal skills or the lack thereof. Sometimes bullying or other conflicts occur, and the school setting can make these issues easier to identify for the mentor.

Fourth, resources such as computers, libraries, gyms and school grounds can serve to make a more comfortable mentoring environment, particularly in the early stages of a relationship. Looking something up on the internet, reading a book together, shooting baskets, or going for a walk on the playground can often break the ice early on, and sometimes these are good ways of varying established mentoring relationships as well.

Fifth, there is a TeamMates coordinator in every school building. This person helps make the mentoring match by pairing mentors and mentees who have similar interests. The coordinator also makes sure that there is a place and time to meet, keeps track of the number of times the mentor and mentee meet and serves as a resource if the mentor or the student have concerns about how the match is going.

Sixth, since a school-based setting makes for a more secure mentoring environment, liability insurance rates are lower. Our average cost per match is a little less than $400 per student per year. Annual costs per match for most mentoring programs range between $1,000–$2,000 per year. We are able to reach many more young people due to these lower costs.

I have mentored three young men through formal Team-Mates matches over the past eighteen years. I started mentoring the first young man during his seventh grade year and stayed with him through the conclusion of his senior year of high school.

He failed to graduate on time from high school, and I felt I had failed as a mentor. However, a few years after he left high school he called me and wanted me to come and visit his family, as his daughter had just had her first birthday. He was working two jobs to provide for his family and had completed his GED, so he did have a high school education. I believe his calling me and wanting me to see his family and his telling me about the effort he had made to finish high school indicated that he saw some value in our relationship. He appreciated me sticking with him through difficult times. This was not a storybook mentoring relationship, but I believe this young man is now a productive member of society and having had a mentor was a positive factor in his life.

My second TeamMate and I started meeting in his ninth grade year. I was in Congress during our years together, but I would see him on Mondays before I flew to Washington or on Fridays when I got back, and we had a good relationship.

He was a good athlete, graduated on time and earned a football scholarship at a medium-sized college. He didn't enjoy college, however, and quit school after his first year to join the Marines, serving in the Middle-East conflict. He had a tour of duty in Iraq and a second tour in Afghanistan, where he experienced a significant amount of fighting against the Taliban in the mountains. He is now out of the service, has a family and is planning on finishing his education. I call him once or twice a year, and I am proud of what he has accomplished.

My third mentee and I were matched through TeamMates while he was in the fourth grade. I have been his mentor for eight years now. He is on track to graduate from high school and plans to go to college. He is formulating his career plans, and I think he will do well with his life. He is a hard worker, has been a good citizen, and has been a pleasure to work with. Research has shown the longer the mentoring match the more positive the results, and that has been the case with this relationship. We know each other well and have come to understand our respective strengths and idiosyncrasies. I am sure we will stay in touch for many years.

Having had personal experience as a mentor, having benefited from working with many mentors through TeamMates, and having had the benefit of studying a large body of research concerning mentoring, I will make some observations regarding what I believe to be the best practices of mentoring.

Role Model

Mentors are often referred to as role models. I don't believe this means the mentor should seek to make the mentee a carbon copy of himself or herself. Rather I believe the mentor should model certain behaviors which lead to strong character and will serve the mentee well for a lifetime. For example, a good mentor is one who is consistent and reliable. If the mentor keeps commitments and is on time, this serves as a great example to the mentee. If the mentor is always truthful and keeps promises, this models integrity and integrity builds trust. If the mentor maintains proper confidentiality the mentee realizes that things which are discussed with the mentor will not be used in ways that could be hurtful to the mentee.

Serving as a role model does not mean the mentor tries to influence the young person to have the same hobbies, read the same books, enter the same profession, or walk, talk and dress like the mentor. The mentor's primary responsibility is to help the mentee become what the mentee hopes and dreams to be. By modeling sound character, the mentor provides the mentee with an example of a pattern of behavior which helps the young person be successful in achieving his or her hopes and dreams. The mentor does not model exactly *what* the mentee needs to be, rather the mentor models *how* the mentee can accomplish her goals by having good values and sound character.

Developmental Mentoring

It is important to let the mentee take the lead in determining what happens in the mentoring session. Some young people like to play board games; some like to shoot baskets or toss a football; some just want to talk. The mentor can suggest an activity, but it is important for each session to revolve around the mentee's interests.

I recall visiting with a mentor who was frustrated with his mentoring experience. He was a very achievement oriented individual and was intent on "fixing" his mentee. Each week he presented a list of things for his mentee to accomplish. It was obvious to the mentor what the mentee's deficiencies were, and he set about making changes in an authoritarian manner. As might be expected, the young person did not appreciate this dictatorial approach and the relationship did not go well.

At times the mentor may need to provide guidance without being overbearing. For example, if the mentee has many absences from school, the mentor might engage the mentee in a discussion of what the mentee wants to be doing in ten years or twenty years. Usually the long term plan the young person discusses will involve education in order to achieve the desired result. The mentor can then help the mentee see more clearly the connection between regular school attendance and achieving those long-term goals through academic achievement.

When the young person arrives at a decision on his own that getting to school on time with regularity is in his best interest, he is going to be much more likely to follow through. You may recall the conversation the mentor had with her mentee concerning the honor roll. The young lady did not know what the honor roll was, so the mentor explained and shared that those on the honor roll were in school every day. This led to the mentee deciding that being on the honor roll was a good thing, which caused her to attend school every day, but it was her decision, not the mentor's.

Developmental mentoring seeks to help the mentee grow into that which he hopes to become. Authoritarian mentoring seeks to cause the mentee to become what the mentor wants him to become. A developmental approach works much better.

Listening

We have mentioned previously that listening carefully to the mentee is crucial in the mentoring relationship. It is important for the mentor to be fully present, focusing exclusively on the mentee and what he or she is communicating. This is much easier said than done. We are a multi-tasking, somewhat distracted society. We scan text messages while appearing to listen to others, watch television while conversing. We carry on conversations at a social event while glancing about the room to see whom we should be meeting and greeting next.

It is relatively rare to focus exclusively on one person for any length of time. Yet giving another our undivided attention is a powerful gift. It tells the other person they are important, that their opinion matters. It builds another's self-worth and sense of well-being. As has been mentioned earlier, many parents have been surprised at how effective giving their own children a block of time in which they are completely focused on their child can be. They realize what makes a difference in mentoring also makes a difference in parenting. It is easy for families to go for days without genuine dialogue and interaction. We are too busy doing "important" things.

It is essential to not just listen to the mentee's words. Visual cues such as eyes tearing up, body language, and tone of voice, often communicate in ways which words do not. Mentoring, at its best, requires the mentor's total attention.

Non-judgmental

It is also important to avoid judging the content of what the mentee says. When what the mentee says is criticized, laughed at, or rejected it won't be long before communication shuts down. If the mentor listens in a non-judgmental way and reflects back or clarifies what the mentee is saying, the mentee is often able to analyze what he is communicating in a constructive manner. For example, a young man might say "I hate my parents." The mentor might reply, "it seems that you are very angry with your parents." The mentee might then say, "yes, I really get upset when they won't let me play some of my video games." The mentor might then say, "your parents limit which video games you can play?" The mentee might then respond that his parents think that some video games are bad for him and hinder his mental development. Eventually the conversation leads the mentee to realize even though he is upset about not being allowed to play certain video games, this is being done out of concern for his well-being, because his parents love him and want the best for him.

The mentor has not criticized the mentee's original statement by saying something such as, "you shouldn't hate your parents." Rather, by reflecting back and clarifying what the mentee has said, the mentor enables the young man to work through his anger and come to a better understanding of why he is frustrated, ultimately realizing his parents are trying to care for him, not control him. Mentoring requires skill and a certain amount of restraint and patience. Young people usually come to the point where they make good decisions if the mentor engages in a way which is caring and without judgment.

Mentors are never perfect. We all make mistakes. If the mentee knows the mentor's heart is in the right place, the mentor truly wants the best for the mentee, and the mentor accepts the mentee with "unconditional positive regard" (agape love), the mentee will look past occasional missteps and bond with the mentor. Giving the young person undivided attention and listening without judging are evidences that the mentor truly cares about the mentee and has the mentee's best interests at heart.

Parents

The role parents play in the mentoring relationship is also very important. We never enroll a young person in the Team-Mates program if the young person or her parents don't want to have her in it. Many parents realize a mentor can provide an important extra dimension to their child's life and are totally on board. I have had many parents thank me for the influence mentoring has had on their child. It is rare to find a parent who refuses to have a child be mentored.

It is essential parents are supportive of the mentoring relationship, and it is equally important that the mentor is aware he or she is not replacing the parent, but rather is an added resource for the young person. It is also important that the mentor does not strike up a relationship with parents, which can cause the young person to feel "ganged up on" by the mentor and parents. The parents may want the mentor to say certain things or reinforce an agenda they have tried to implement with their child. If the mentee senses the mentor is acting as an agent of his or her parents the relationship will be jeopardized.

Confidentiality

As mentioned earlier, the mentor-mentee relationship is heavily dependent on confidentiality. If the mentee tells the mentor something in confidence and it gets back to the mentee through parents, teachers or classmates, the mentoring relationship will be damaged. Trust will have been broken, and the mentee will no longer want to share anything of significance with the mentor. The mentor must walk a fine line. It is important to have a good relationship with parents and school personnel, but at the same time not betray a confidence.

Vision and Strengths

A vision of what the mentee hopes to become is usually related to the strengths the young person possesses. As my friend Dr. Don Clifton observed many years ago, a person is most successful when the role they play is based upon their unique talents. The mentor can be of great service to the mentee by helping the mentee better understand his strengths, those gifts he has which are unique and enduring. Assessing strengths may best be done by providing a formal index, such as Strengths Finder through Gallup or other such indices.

The mentor also can identify strengths through observation. You may recall my grandfather's mentor, Currens, heard my grandfather give a speech when my grandfather was in elementary school and determined that my grandfather had a real gift for public speaking. Currens believed my grandfather could use that strength in the ministry and Currens' vision and encouragement led to my grandfather pursuing a college education, then going to seminary and becoming a preacher.

If the mentor is able to recognize and identify strengths and then present possible ways in which those strengths might be used in the future, the mentee often gravitates toward a future path which engages his strengths and his passion. The vision must be shaped and accepted by the mentee, but the mentor can be instrumental in pointing out possible ways in which the mentee's unique talents can be used. The mentor is often able to encourage the mentee to explore educational options, those schools and those academic majors which best utilize the mentee's talents. Also the mentor can sometimes point out summer employment or internships which lead to job opportunities which engage the unique talents of the mentee.

Hope

All of us are shaped by our past experience. Patterns of behavior often become cyclical, as one comes to expect the future to hold what has been experienced in the past.

A mentor can be an enormous help in changing negative expectations, expectations which often become self-fulfilling prophesies. The mentor, by pointing out strengths the mentee has, but often isn't aware of, can enable the mentee to see beyond her present circumstance. The mentor, by pointing out future possibilities, can enable the mentee to see light at the end of the tunnel, a future which is unlike what the mentee has grown up with. The mentor can aid in guiding the young person through the necessary steps toward a better future.

A person without hope often fills his life with destructive patterns of behavior. One who is hopeful about the future is proactive, positive and goal-oriented. Providing a greater sense of hope is one of the most powerful benefits of mentoring.

Altruism

It has been interesting to talk to many TeamMates mentees who have graduated from high school and gone on to college. The majority of these students indicate they want to be mentors. After having experienced the love and acceptance of a mentor for an extended period of time, they want to give the same gift to another young person.

It seems when a mentor gives the gift of time and consistent support to one who, on the surface of things, can give nothing back in return, the mentee experiences firsthand the power of unconditional love and acceptance. The infusion of such caring over time gives the mentee self-worth and the desire to help someone else in return. Those who have been cared for want to care for others. Mentoring causes a positive ripple effect and short circuits the transmission of negative energy. This is important to the preservation of our culture.

Mentor Training and Development

I do a great deal of mentor recruiting. I have found prospective mentors can present many reasons they shouldn't become mentors. One might think the primary reason people would give for not choosing to become a mentor would be lack of time. In many cases this reason is given, but we have found the most common reason people don't become mentors is fear of failure. They are apprehensive about their ability to be a good mentor, to relate to a young person who is a complete stranger.

We have found a comprehensive mentor training program dispels many of the concerns about being inadequate as a mentor. TeamMates requires a two hour training session for all new mentors. A great deal of information is packed into those two hours.

Training often begins with a discussion of the developmental stages young people go through as they move from elementary school to middle school then on to high school. There are physical, emotional and intellectual changes which occur through each stage, and it is important for the mentor to adapt mentoring sessions so what transpires is appropriate for each age level. For example, elementary school students are not as concerned about peer pressures as middle school students, and middle school students are becoming aware of the opposite sex, but not as aware as high school students. Elementary school students may enjoy playing board games, middle school students may be interested in exploring topics with their mentors on the internet, and high school students may be more interested in engaging in dialogue about dating, college choices, or career aspirations. No two students are exactly alike, but the mentor needs to realize that mentoring will need to take on a different complexion as students mature.

Training emphasizes the importance of confidentiality. There is one exception to maintaining a high level of confidentiality. If the mentee is being abused or is a danger to himself or others, the mentor is required by law to report this information to appropriate authorities. Contact information for appropriate reporting is furnished at the training session. Many tragic events reported in the news each day could have been prevented if the young person involved had been in a good mentoring relationship.

Boundaries are also important in the mentoring relationship. Guidelines for physical touching and hugging are discussed. It is generally better to err on the side of caution, particularly during the early stages of the relationship.

Even though mentoring occurs in a school setting, mentors are encouraged to keep the door open and the shades open if meeting with the mentee in a separate room. Since school-based mentoring usually occurs in a library, cafeteria, a bench in the hallway, or on school grounds, such precautions are normally not necessary.

Mentors cannot interact with mentees on Facebook, Twitter or other social media outlets, which are open to public scrutiny. Information which is private and confidential between the mentor and mentee can sometimes be revealed.

Sometimes children will request money, food or gifts. More often, the mentor will want to give the mentee something when they see a need, but we find doing so often changes the mentoring relationship from that of mentoring to the mentor's being seen as a source of material gifts. Mentors are encouraged to provide information and guidance concerning where the mentee's needs can be met. This may mean helping the young person get connected with tutoring if she is not doing well in a subject, ensuring the mentee gets involved with a backpack program or a food bank if there are hunger issues, and visiting with the school nurse or other health organizations if there are medical needs. The mentor needs to be seen as a wise counselor, not the bearer of gifts.

Role playing is used extensively in mentor training. The mentor may be asked what he or she would do in the following situations: the mentee is having trouble with fractions and asks the mentor for help, the mentee reports that he is being bullied on Facebook and wants to know what to do, a mentee reports that her mother humiliates her in front of others and asks for advice. Of course there are many scenarios which can be presented and no training session can cover every possible mentoring dilemma, but the mentor being trained can begin to think through the appropriate mentoring response in many diverse situations.

Mentor training also involves a discussion of cultural differences. Mentoring can be effective across cultures, but the mentor must be aware of cultural differences before he can appropriately deal with them. Styles of dress, types of food eaten, and values vary from one culture to another and the more aware that the mentor is of the differences, the better the relationship with the mentee.

It is very important the mentor understands the difference between prescriptive, authoritarian mentoring and developmental mentoring. A prescriptive mentor usually has his own agenda and is focused on what he wants to accomplish in the relationship. A prescriptive mentor dominates the conversation and does very little listening, gives advice, solves the mentees' problems and often judges the correctness or incorrectness of what the mentee says.

A developmental mentor focuses on the mentee and what

the mentee desires, listens carefully, helps guide the mentee toward arriving at her own solutions to her problems, and makes it apparent the mentor is there to help the mentee develop into all that she can be. Obviously, mentor training seeks to distinguish between prescriptive and developmental approaches to mentoring and encourages the mentor to avoid prescriptive practices and to use developmental skills in mentoring.

Mentor training does not end with the initial two hour training session. We believe it is important to familiarize mentors with the latest mentoring research via email and our web site. Every three years mentors are required to go through a re-training process. The re-training is shorter but is a refresher that contains new information which research and our experience have revealed to be important in mentoring.

We also provide opportunities for mentors to get together to share ideas and concerns. Often hearing that other mentors encounter many of the same issues with their mentees is encouraging, as the mentor often thinks she was the only one experiencing such issues. Hearing what others have done in similar situations is helpful. Additionally, the TeamMates school building facilitator is available for advice and support and has expertise in dealing with a wide variety of situations mentors encounter.

Research has shown the longer the mentoring relationship lasts, the more positive the outcomes. As has been mentioned, the average TeamMates match currently lasts for thirty six months, or three years. This compares favorably to a national average length of match of less than one year. Many mentors are with their mentee for eight or nine years, having started with their mentee in the third or fourth grade and maintaining the match through high school graduation. Some even continue with their mentee as a post-secondary mentor for those high school graduates who are first-generation college students.

No match lasts forever. Part of mentor training involves a

discussion of how to best end a match. If the mentor is moving away, has had a significant change in job responsibilities, or incurs health issues which have made it impossible to continue with the match, it is important to give the mentee notice of the change well in advance.

Above all, it is important for the mentee to understand the match is not ending because the mentee is at fault or the mentor just doesn't care about the mentee. The mentor can assure the mentee the match is ending because of unavoidable circumstances and the mentor still cares about the mentee very much and wants the best for him. If the mentor can be actively engaged in recruiting a new mentor and introduce the new mentor to the mentee, it can be very helpful.

We can see that properly preparing the mentor and the mentee before the match is made is very important to the quality of the match and the length of the match. Ongoing support of mentors is also very important. If mentors feel they are surrounded by people who care about them and their mentee and are willing to devote resources to sustaining and strengthening the match, it makes a great deal of difference.

A final thought. No country is more than one generation away from serious decline. The best way to protect the nation is to ensure the nation's young people are properly equipped to be responsible and productive citizens. Mentoring serves as a powerful instrument to nurture young people so they can realize their full potential and contribute to the common good. If we fail to invest time, love and guidance in our children we do so at our own peril.

Together We Transform Lives

TeamMates has been mentioned throughout this book, so I am certain the reader has some understanding of TeamMates at this point. However, it is often easier to understand an organization better if one has an explanation of how it began and what the vision for the organization is going forward.

TeamMates had its beginnings in 1991. I came home from football practice one evening and my wife, Nancy, was excited about a television program she had just watched. The episode involved an elderly gentleman named Eugene Lang who had been asked to speak at the graduation exercises of the elementary school he had attended many years before.

Upon arriving at the school, East Harlem Public School 121, Mr. Lang was surprised at the changes which had occurred, not just the aging of the school building, but the changes within the student body. When he had attended the school it was located in the suburbs and was in a fairly nice area. Now, however, it was part of the inner city and the children attending the school were from much more diverse backgrounds than when Eugene had attended. He also was struck by the fact that many of the students were apparently from impoverished circumstances. He asked the principal how many of the students would likely attend college and the principal told him maybe one would.

Eugene had gone to Swarthmore at the age of fifteen. He had been successful in the business world, developing several patents on ATM machines, credit card and bar code technology, and had become wealthy. So, when confronted by the changes within the student body before him, he told the students if they would stay out of trouble and graduate from high school he would pay their way to college. Eventually ninety percent of those children graduated from high school and half went on to prestigious universities.

Nancy was impressed by what Eugene Lang had done and asked if there was something we might do of a similar nature. I told her I wasn't prepared to put an entire elementary school through college at that time but would see what we might do.

I had been troubled by the changes in family stability I had seen in the lives of many of my players over the years and had already given some thought to what might be done to provide more support to young people. The next day, in a team meeting, I asked our players if any of them would be willing to spend time mentoring some young men from Lincoln schools. Twenty two players raised their hands indicating a willingness to serve as mentors.

We then approached administrators in the Lincoln school system to see if they would be interested in having some football players work with twenty two seventh and eighth grade boys who would like to have a mentor. The matches were made in a rather random manner. We had no idea what we were doing. We told the players to spend some time with their mentees every week. We also got the players and the mentees together once a month to play basketball, have a speaker, and provide some pizza and soft drinks.

Things seemed to be going well. Nancy and a lady from the Lincoln schools named Barb Hopkins attended to most of the details. After a couple of years I began to be a little uneasy, however, as some of the young men were now approaching the age of sixteen, an age at which they could choose to drop out of school.

We got the mentees and their parents together and made the Eugene Lang promise. If they would stay in school and stay out of trouble, we would see to it that their college education would be paid for. There was one minor difficulty with this promise–I had no idea where the money was going to come from.

Fortunately, a few years earlier, some Nebraska fans had observed that Bob Devaney's teams had won one hundred games, and the teams I had coached had won one hundred games, so they had a "Double 100" celebration and raised some money which was deposited in the University of Nebraska Foundation. It turned out that this money could be used for college expenses for the young men in the organization we now called TeamMates. Needless to say, I breathed a sigh of relief when I found out about the fund and the way in which it could be used.

As time went on, the twenty two mentees became high school seniors. Those we had selected in 1991 as eighth graders reached senior status in the 1995-96 school year and those who had begun the program as seventh graders were seniors in 1996-97. We found that twenty one of the original twenty two mentees graduated on schedule, which was pleasing and somewhat surprising. What was even more surprising was eighteen of the twenty two went on to post-secondary education. Some went to community colleges, and many went on to four year colleges. These results far exceeded our expectations for this particular group of young men.

Currently we have a robust scholarship program that serves those mentees going on to college. However, with the large number of young people we are currently serving, we are not able to provide full scholarships as we did for the original group of mentees.

Because of our brief foray into the field of mentoring, and because this journey seemed to have yielded excellent results, we decided to expand the program for the 1997 school year. We recruited one hundred and sixty volunteers from Lincoln to serve as mentors. We realized we weren't going to have enough football players to mentor large numbers of young people. We also realized that college students will often not be able to form long-term mentoring relationships because of their four year college careers. Therefore, we began to recruit adults as mentors and began to mentor young women as well as young men.

At first we stayed with the original model of starting with seventh and eighth graders, but we soon realized many decisions were made before the seventh grade that often had life-long consequences. Decisions concerning drugs and alcohol, what kinds of people to form friendships with, and decisions about the importance of education can start a young person on a path which is difficult to alter. Therefore we lowered the age at which we would begin mentoring to the third grade. We find that by the third grade a young person is able to carry on a conversation with an adult and form a relationship. As mentioned previously, a TeamMates mentor can begin mentoring at many age levels, but third grade is the earliest. Some people are more comfortable with a middle school or high school student, but most prefer to start with a younger child. The longer the match lasts, the better the outcome, so starting early and maintaining the match through high school graduation or beyond is optimal.

In 1998 we decided to expand TeamMates across the state of Nebraska. With the help of Senator Bob Kerrey we received a federal grant which enabled us to help pay for the start-up costs in many small communities across the state. By the end of the 1998-1999, school year we had established twelve chapters with four hundred forty one matches.

Larger communities such as Lincoln and Omaha have many different mentoring programs. However, most small communities had no mentoring program. I recall participating in a hearing in the Nebraska State Legislature in which mentoring was being discussed. A state senator from a rural area told me mentoring was not necessary in small Nebraska towns as there was no need for mentoring programs in rural Nebraska. Apparently he was of the opinion that young people in rural areas had no challenges in their lives. I didn't argue with him, but the data we possess indicates he was very wrong.

In most rural Nebraska areas TeamMates is the only mentoring program available. We have found the response in most of these communities has been overwhelmingly favorable. Some small communities with only a few hundred residents mentor as many as one hundred children. Such communities take a great deal of pride in the investment they are making in their young people.

TeamMates has continued to grow at a rate of approximately sixteen percent annually for the last several years and we enter the 2015 school year with approximately 7,500 matches in 133 communities. Fourteen of the communities are in Iowa, one is in San Diego, California, and the remaining 118 are in Nebraska.

We have reduced the annual cost per mentoring match from more than $500 to less than $400. At the same time we have managed to improve the quality of our matches and the effectiveness of the program. The addition of focusing on strengths which mentees possess as well as providing post-secondary mentors for first-generation college students has made TeamMates unique in the mentoring world.

We also attempt to provide mentors for all young people who want a mentor, not just for those who might be labeled "at-risk." The "at-risk" label is very subjective and often misleading. Every young person is at some risk, but at the same time every young person has potential and is capable of doing great things. Providing a mentor usually tips the scales in the direction of positive outcomes.

As previously stated, the average TeamMate match length of thirty six months far exceeds the national average, and the advantages we see in a school-based mentoring program have been documented. We are trying to ensure the viability of Team-Mates in future years by building an endowment through the TeamMates Foundation.

Our vision is "to become the gold standard of school-based mentoring, and to serve 12,000 youth by 2020." This is an ambitious goal but one that we are intent upon achieving. At the present time, TeamMates is one of the largest non-national mentoring programs in the United States.

Given the challenges our young people face, and the fact that there are an estimated sixteen million young people without formal or informal mentors in their lives, the challenges are daunting, the stakes are high, but we can't afford not to try. Above all we can't afford to fail.

Mentoring
Matters
Study Guide

Chapter 1: The Need For Mentors

1. In this chapter, Coach Osborne talks about his experience being fatherless for a period of time. What are some issues you have personally encountered due to fatherlessness?

2. How would say your relationship with your father has impacted the way you lead, parent, or mentor?

3. Who are some of the people you would consider to have played the role of mentor in your life? How did they help you become the person you are today?

4. Where might you have benefitted from the presence of a mentor but did not have one? What did you learn that you could pass on to a young person in a similar situation?

5. What are some specific issues young people are facing in your community?

6. What role do mentors play in addressing some of the issues facing youth in your community?

7. How can you bring more mentors into the lives of youth in your community?

Chapter 2: The Impact of Technology

1. Coach Osborne talks about how technology has changed
    relationships and the way we view the world. In your per-
    sonal experience, what are some major changes you have
    noticed in up-and-coming generations due to technologi-
    cal advances?

2. How much time do you spend (and in what ways) using
    technology? What about your family? What about your
    mentee?

3. Coach Osborne talks about the positive attributes of the
    younger generation. What are some of the positive
    attributes you've observed?

4. In what ways do you see these positive attributes having
    an impact on society?

5. What are some creative ways that you might be able to
    help your mentee use technology for good?

6. What are some things you can do to limit the negative
    impact of technology?

Chapter 3: The Mentor's Key Focus

1. Coach Osborne talks about some negative influences of our culture on young people. In your experience, what poses the greatest threat to young people today?

2. What does the phrase "unconditional love" mean to you?

3. What are some ways unconditional love shows up in a mentoring relationship?

4. How do you think showing unconditional love might impact a young person's sense of hope?

5. Coach Osborne talks about how he pushed his son away from skateboarding. He opines that a mentor, being removed from the situation, might have encouraged the activity and seen value in it. What talent or special interests do you see in your mentee that other adults might miss or discourage?

6. In what ways can you help your mentee use those talents and interests to benefit others around them?

Chapter 4: Strengths and Affirmation

1. Think back to your childhood and teenage years. Who were some of the people that encouraged you? What specific words of affirmation did they use?

2. Did you have any negative voices speak into your life? Do those words still affect you today or have you been able to move past it?

3. Coach Osborne talks about how encouragement and affirmation can help an average athlete become great. Give an example of a time you achieved more than you thought you were capable through someone else's affirmation.

4. How can you affirm and encourage your mentee?

5. In what ways can you help build a network of affirmation and support for your mentee?

6. What can you and your mentee to together to create a culture of meaningful affirmation in the school or community?

Chapter 5: My Grandfather's Story

1. Coach Osborne shares a story about how one man helped change the trajectory of his grandfather's life. Do you have any stories similar to the one Coach Osborne shared?

2. How often do you think about the events that led to you being where you are today? In what ways do you think your life could be different based on the decisions of your ancestors?

3. What are some of your strengths? Did you always know you had those strengths or did someone else help you make that discovery?

4. What are your mentees strengths? How did you learn to recognize them as strengths?

5. Do you easily recognize strengths in others or is it something at which you have to work? What steps do you usually take when trying to discover those strengths?

6. What are some things you can do today that will help you become more intentional in your search for the strengths in others?

Chapter 6: The Importance of Meaning and Purpose

1. Share a difficult experience in which people were able to overcome their circumstance to find meaning and purpose.

2. Can you describe a time when you were generally happy about your life but still lacked a sense of meaning and purpose?

3. How has mentoring provided a sense of meaning and purpose to your life?

4. How does serving others help you deal with difficulties in your own life?

5. How could you encourage your mentee to serve others? What projects could you do together to encourage this practice?

6. How can you help your mentee explore what his or her purpose might be right now? What about in the future?

Chapter 7: Coaching and Mentoring

1. What do you think is the most important role of the coach in today's society?

2. Who are some of the coaches or mentors that you remember most and why?

3. What are some specific ways your coaches or mentors impacted your life both positively and negatively?

4. As a mentor, what do you think are the most important lessons you should try to pass down to your mentee?

5. How important is consistency when it comes to mentoring? What about the way you model work ethic?

6. How do you generally deal with adversity? In what ways can you help your mentee deal with adversity?

7. Coach Osborne tells the story about former Nebraska quarterback Brook Berringer. Have you been around a person who had this type of impact on others?

8. Coach Osborne talks about "transactional" leadership and "transformational" leadership. How is mentoring like transformational leadership and how is it different?

Chapter 8: Post-Secondary Mentoring

1. Coach Osborne talks about the primary stages of youth: elementary, middle school, high school, and post-secondary. Which of those four times in your life was the most important to your overall development?

2. What have you observed about how mentoring can be helpful within each time period of a young person's life?

3. Do you think there is a greater need for post-secondary mentoring today than in previous eras?

4. What are some of the big decisions a high school graduate or college student might be required to make? What are some factors in a young person's life that might make those decisions easier or more difficult?

5. What do you think are some of the benefits a young adult might receive from having a mentor throughout the early years of their post-secondary life?

6. What are some of your past experiences that you feel might benefit a post-secondary mentee?

7. What are some of the challenges that might exist in this kind of mentoring relationship? In what ways might you need to be more intentional in your approach to mentoring a young adult as opposed to an elementary, middle school or high school student?

Chapter 9: Informal Mentoring

1. Coach Osborne cites a study in which 80 percent of unemployed, non-students from the ages of 16-24 desired a mentor in their lives. Why do you think that number is so high? How do you think young people in that situation might benefit from mentoring?

2. How would you define the concept of "informal mentoring?"

3. Who have been some of your informal mentors? How would you describe the impact they had on your life? Did you realize they were mentoring you at the time or is that something you came to understand later on?

4. In what ways are you informally mentoring young people and adults in your life?

5. How can you encourage your mentee to become an informal mentor to others?

6. What are the benefits of a formal mentoring relationship for a young person? What are the benefits of an informal relationship?

Chapter 10: Effective Mentoring Practices

1. Coach Osborne shares three personal mentoring stories that all have very different circumstances and varying outcomes. Can you relate to any of those stories? Why or why not?

2. In what ways do you think Coach Osborne's experiences expose the need for more committed mentors?

3. Coach Osborne lists several keys to effective mentoring: acting as a role model, utilizing developmental tactics as a mentor, listening, being non-judgmental, parental involvement, confidentiality, having vision and understanding strengths, giving hope, encouraging altruism, and personal training and development. Which of these do you find most natural to incorporate as a mentor? Which of these do you find most difficult?

4. How would you prioritize the keys to effective mentoring? Which are most important?

5. Coach Osborne talks about altruism and the concept of instilling the desire to serve within the person being mentored. Do you have any examples of someone you have mentored that went on to serve others as a mentor or in some other capacity? If so, how did that make you feel about your commitment to that individual?

6. How can you encourage other mentors in your community? What can you do together to become better mentors?